Adaptive Coaching for Leaders

Developing Talent in Others

Bill Winfrey

First Printing: 2021

Bill Winfrey Training Publications

Apex, NC 27502

ISBN# 978-1-7361729-0-2

Adaptive Coaching for Leaders: options / companion materials

In person
- workshops
  - participant workbooks
  - leader's guide with ppt slide deck
  - Adaptive Coach – 360 (feedback tool)
- coaching

Distance
- online workshops
- online coaching
- self-paced e-learning
- Adaptive Coaching – 360 (feedback tool)

Other
- Adaptive Coaching & DISC Styles
- Adaptive Coaching App

See www.AdaptiveTeamLeadership.com

Dedication

to my wife
Dr. Nancy Vigander Winfrey

She's been the light of my life now for over 35 years, but she has become a shining example to many others as an active community servant and as a dedicated lifelong learner. She created and ran a non-profit that supported a grassroots school in Guatemala City for 14 years, until violence forced the school to close. In midlife, she completed a masters and a PhD in Adult Education ... all while working full time and continuing to love and care for her family. She has been a very insightful sounding board on any subject matter I present, and this book is much improved from her thoughts and insights. I am very fortunate.

Acknowledgement

a friend and mentor
Bill Delano

For many years I've had the good fortune to work with and learn from this master trainer, facilitator, and OD practicianer. Bill is the founder and director of Triangle Training Center outside of Chapel Hill, NC. His passion for excellence, his expertise in his field, and his concern for others have built a company that touches many lives around the globe each year ... including mine. His friendship over the years has been significant in my life and is very appreciated.

Table of Contents

Foreword by Tony Alessandra, PhD

In *Adaptive Coaching for Leaders (AC)*, Bill Winfrey provides an insightful and intuitive framework to help you further apply the Platinum Rule®, by coaching others based on their needs, not yours.

Teams and companies rise or fall based on the quality of individual contributions. Leadership success is thus intricately connected to an ability to coach, to impact performance.

But good performance coaching is not a particular style; it's more about reading and responding well to shifting needs. The challenges of a beginner are much different than those of a high performer, or from someone who has regressed. When coaches default to the style they're most comfortable with, they only randomly fit the real need of the moment. More often they miss the mark or even hinder.

Adaptive Coaching for Leaders will guide you to adapt appropriately to changing scenarios, and then give you a logical system for managing performance over time. You'll clarify roles, key tasks, and expectations. You'll agree on performance levels and their naturally corresponding coaching styles. Coach and co-worker will both benefit from fewer surprises and increased engagement.

My life's work has been helping leaders and co-workers be more effective by adapting to the real needs of others through applying the Platinum Rule®. *Adaptive Coaching for Leaders* is in that same lane. It will be a valuable tool in helping you become a more others-centered leader, a proven trait of great leaders.

Tony Alessandra, PhD … author of 32 books including:
- *The Platinum Rule®*
- *The NEW Art of Managing People*
- *Communicating at Work*

Introduction

leaders are coaches

Leadership is a broad concept, but fundamentally its job is to get results ... usually measured as a team output. Because team success is dependent upon individual contributions, the ability to coach individuals becomes intricate to both team and leadership success.

one size does not fit all

Coaching is more than just demanding results. It's meeting them where they are and skillfully offering what is most needed. That means flexing to shifting needs, not coaching to our own preference. A one size fits all approach will randomly be a good fit, maybe a third of the time. Yet between 'hands on', 'hand-in', and 'hand off' coaching styles ... needs differ and mismatches are not just ineffective, they're an obstacle.

> "Fairness is giving all people the treatment they earn and deserve. It doesn't mean treating everyone alike."
>
> John Wooden
> 1910 – 2010
> UCLA basketball coach

Adaptive Coaching is not new

Adaptive Coaching (AC) captures and simplifies what we are doing when we're at our best. It then offers a logical framework to help you continue to adjust and convert your intuition into applied wisdom.

It draws on timeless insights, and thus you'll find a number of quotes reflecting similar observations from different periods and places.

It's not a magic formula, but rather a compass to point you in the right direction. As you then inject your own heart, soul, and experience ... you may well become someone's Coach of the Year.

.

Clarifications

coach vs leader ... in this book, a coach is someone leading an individual and a leader is generally leading a group.

coach / coaching ... I will use these terms in a broader sense than most tend to use in a business setting. I'll draw from how the terms are used in athletics, where a coach is a large role that uses a wide range of interactions. So I'm not using it as one particular style of leading but rather as a larger role that draws upon a continuum of styles ... from hands-on, to hand-in, to hand-off.

co-worker ... Refers to the person being coached. I preferred this term over terms like employee, coachee, or follower.

Raeb ... a middle-age Reflective Transformational Philosopher, lived in mid-eastern hilly region of Chapalil, later Toun-ova Pecs

action icon ... This represents an opportunity to stop and take action to put a concept into pratice.

Action!

many quotes ... You will notice a lot of quotes throughout. That goes with the basic idea that these concepts are nothing new, but enduring truths that have been observed and commented on by people from many walks of life over a long period of time.

2 sections of the book ... You'll see in the TOC 2 halves. The first, **Fundamentals of Performance** (Parts 1 & 2) ... is on the basics of making changes, the ground floor of any performance improvement. These principles will become the foundation of the AC model. The second half, **AC Application** (Parts 3 & 4) builds the AC model in a logical and progressive way, then gets into how to apply it.

Part 1

Things Connected

A model is a model if it's a valuable guide. But understanding the principles behind it enables you to fill in gaps and make needed adjustments. Parts 1 and 2 are about the principles from which the AC model comes.

1 Actions Produce Results

What if you and I had a superpower?

Not a pretend one from the comic books ... but a very practical and effective one. And more specifically, what if our power was the ability to bring into our lives whatever we think?

Just imagine how amazing that ability would be. We'd for sure be achieving big goals and experiencing the very best life has to offer.

Well, according to generations of writers, philosophers, counselors, observant life travelers, etc ... we surely do possess that very ability.

Throughout written history, humans have continually rediscovered the very direct connection between how we think and what materializes in our lives. It's a connection that often goes unnoticed, but is at work regardless.

So, according to these sages, we're way more powerful than we realize.

actions are our real power

When Dorothy discovered Oz pulling levers behind the curtain she was shocked to realize his super powers were nothing mystical. And neither are ours.

> "You create the results in life that you believe you deserve."
>
> Dr. Phil McGraw
> 1950 –
> author, psychologist

Ours are rooted in basic principles that we both engage and overlook every day. Principles like, we reap what we sow, or that for every action there is an equal and opposite reaction.

These type truths mean that throughout our lives, even our micro-actions are causing micro-results that continue to accumulate. Their results don't love us or hate us, nor are they for us or against us. They are simply the unbiased effect of causes we've set in motion.

So, it's valid to look at the life we are experiencing now (material surroundings, finances, relationships, etc) not so much as a success or failure, but rather as the impartial consequences of our countless choices and actions. We're objectively reaping what we have sown. If we want different results, that will simply require different actions.

While our power is not supernatural, it still is super powerful. We carry the great ability to cause things to happen, to create change on whatever we're willing to act upon. Sometimes we surprise ourselves and accomplish way more than we thought we could. But we do not accomplish way more than is consistent with our actions.

> "You've always had the power my dear, you just had to learn it for yourself."
>
> Glinda, the good witch

actions matter

This physical world we were born into is one impacted by action ... not by intentions or potential or hopes or wishes ... but actions.

HERE LIES
KUDA BENGRATE

BORN 1908
DIED 1980

Almost wrote 5
best selling books

No one benefits from books I almost wrote. No hungry person is fed by my good intentions. No discouraged friend is comforted by my plans to reach out that never materialize.

When we reflect on a life in review ... we admire what was accomplished, not what they never quite got around to. On tombstones we chisel actual results ... not potential. And while we often judge ourselves by our intentions, others judge us by our actions and results ... and we view them just the same. It's our actions that write the scripts of our lives and cement our legacies. Our intentions and our faith are both dead without them.

"May the work I've done speak for me."

Elijah Cummings
1951 – 2019
US congressman

The difference between intentions and actions is the difference between a great trip considered versus a great trip experienced.

A simple action is worth 1000 intentions.

actions build us inwardly too

Actions are also a very valuable power source for internal health and change. Possessions and unearned success can puff us up, but actions toward meaningful goals can't help but build self-esteem and confidence. The reverse is also true, and is seen when retirees become inactive. Their loss of activity toward meaningful goals affects the whole person, sometimes initiating a dangerous downward spiral.

I'm responsible

Because our actions bring results ... the longer we live, the more responsible we become for what has gathered around us. It's a game changer when we recognize that we create: our physical condition ... our relationships ... our home ... our reputation ... our habits ... our career ... our financial situation, etc. We even teach others how to treat us by what boundaries we accept and enforce.

"Cause an effect."

Raeb

If I'm not where I want to be in certain area of my life, it's easy to create alternative facts that let me off the hook. Illusionary truth may relieve the pain of accountability, but it only delays helpful change.

So, when we realize we're not where we want to be and wonder how we got there, the short answer is the same as the fix ... we got here one day at a time, by unproductive patterns of action. The fix then is to initiate more productive daily patterns.

Let's look at habits a bit.

patterns can make us oblivious

We are creatures of habit, and for good or bad, they build our world. We have habits in every area of life ... eating, exercise, punctuality, money, work, morning, relationships, etc.

"We are what we repeatedly do."

Aristotle
385 BC – 323 BC
Greek philosopher

It's not easy to see the impact of habits. We so easily go on autopilot and disconnect cause and effect. We want to lose weight, but don't see how our diet and exercise patterns are working against us. Or an aspiring athlete who has big time dreams, can't see that his work habits are small-time. Or we treat others at work in an off-putting way which only seems natural to us ... but then wonder why we're not connected to others and not offered an opportunity to advance.

Things go according to our habits ... how we consistently act. Not knowing what habits are producing in our lives is like drinking a chemical solution that we have no idea of what's inside. Patterns can even be killing us softly while we're not paying attention.

My father, for example, began smoking as a young man and soon developed a 3 pack a day habit. In the prime of middle age, he was shocked to find out he had only 50% lung capacity. He enrolled in a 6 month get healthy program at UNC that started with a stress test, which he had to postpone 2 weeks for a business trip. The night before the stress test, he and Mom met family at a restaurant. They arrived early and so went for a short walk to 'prep' for the next morning's test. Afterwards, they returned to the restaurant and sat down with my brother and his future wife. Minutes later he had a massive heart attack ... laughing one minute and gone the next. He had 55 years wonderful years full of love and big accomplishments. We've missed him a lot, and he's missed a lot leaving so soon. He had many good traits and excellent habits, but his health habits got him ... and us.

It takes a lot to be honest with ourselves, to see the impact of our autopilot actions and to then create change. Not everyone gets there.

"People do not decide their futures. They decide their habits and their habits decide their futures."

FM Alexander
1869 – 1955
Australian teacher / actor

not seeing is not believing

It's hard to hit a baseball you can't see, or to change a habit that we don't acknowledge. A lack of clarity stifles action. Others can often see what we are oblivious to. An overweight shopper wonders why in the world they can't drop weight, yet one glance at their grocery cart makes it clear to everyone else.

My friend James, while in the midst of losing a hundred pounds, had a great conversation with a well-known weight loss expert on a plane.

She said she often has friends and family approach her for a bit of free help. Her response is always, "I'd be happy to help, but first write down everything you eat for the next 3 weeks, then contact me." Her goal is for them to connect actions and results.

To her great surprise, she has NEVER gotten a call back after that request. Apparently, that reality check is a significant step.

Not seeing cause and effect stifles change in any area:

- a basketball player I coached gets in foul trouble every game, but continues to blame any and all refs, not seeing that he is the only common denominator

- a friend's drinking patterns began early and then intensified, he later blamed his broken family on everyone but himself

- a high achiever who is self-absorbed, overconfident, and abrasive ... later laments his lack of real connection to others, but has been clueless all along to how others experience him

We spend a lot of money in therapy to connect the dots between cause and effect.

Don't blame others for the road you're on. That's your own asphalt.

a statement I'll never forget

During a challenging time in my life, a friend said something to me that he would never remember, but that I will never forget.

I was about 30 years old and had had a few tough months. Four months prior, my wife's father had passed away after a 9-month battle with cancer. A month later, another heartbreak when we lost my father suddenly to that heart attack. Two months after that our first child was born, which was great ... except for my wife's emergency and 10-day hospital stay that threatened her life. Then I lost my job as part of a lay off ... which began a career change. I was rattled.

I realize others face much greater challenges. These were big for me. I felt numb and was unsure of where I fit in, or what was next. I can tell you exactly where I was when a respected friend caught me off guard by saying ... "What you see, you have created."

Initially I did that dog head tilt thing. I thought, what the heck is that supposed to mean? I said something like ... "This feels out of my control but you're telling me it's my fault?" We kept talking and I saw enough to hang on to the concept for further consideration.

I found he wasn't saying I was responsible for uncontrollable events. But that overall, I do create my world by my actions and my responses. Through one lens his words sounded harsh, but through another ... he was saying I was still in control of where my life heads no matter the tough challenges ... that my thoughts and actions would determine where I go no matter where I am now.

2 Thoughts Produce Actions

I hope these principles sound overly simplistic. While we'll build on them, we won't ever get too far beyond the basics. Expertise in most things is not outgrowing fundamentals, but mastering them.

Last chapter we noted that actions are our power source, and that our results are a direct reflection of our actions.

> "We reap what we sow, and we sow according to what we expect."
>
> Raeb

The point in this chapter is that our actions directly reflect our thoughts, that we act according to our 'faith' … according to what we believe to be possible. I'm not referring to faith in a religious sense, but the principle is true in all of life. If we don't perceive something to be within our sphere of possibility, we instinctively won't act on it.

Our expectations act like a governor on an engine, shrinking or expanding potential. Because our thoughts direct our actions, our inner world creates our outer world. It's how we create self-fulfilling prophesies … both positive or negative.

self-fulfilling prophecies

Our super power is the ability to act and get results. And, because the quality of our thoughts determine the quality of our actions, our super power then is a double-edged sword ... working both for us and against us. Our super power does not filter out the negative. It simply brings whatever we act on, and we act based on how we think.

> "The picture we have of ourselves will always determine how we respond to life."
>
> Myles Munroe
> 1954 – 2014
> Evangelist, Grand Bahama

This means I can be the architect of not only an upward trending spiral, but also a downward one as well ... and I'm responsible for both directions.

> "To think big and to act small is to think small."
>
> Raeb

We've all done it, and we see it all around us ... people following a negative script that's sabotaging their potential ... whether in total, or just in a particular area. Someone may be very successful financially yet be failing to take care of their health or their family relationships. In each case, there's a strong connection between thought and action.

If I believe a certain high standard is beyond me ... my actions will to be consistent with a lower expectation. When my results fall short of the high standard it reenforces my initial belief.

But if I believe that I am capable and worthy of some high standard ... my actions will adjust to be consistent with those beliefs, until results begin to match my expectation. When my results fall short, it's my expectations that jolt me into making some needed adjustment.

we acquire expectations

Regarding expectations, I'm going with concept that we're born 'tabula rasa', a blank slate ... as opposed to being born elite or not ... and that self-perception and personal expectations are then developed from our surroundings and experiences. That doesn't mean we don't come with some hard wiring regarding personality and abilities, but those too will need nurturing to be productive.

> "Failure is a feeling long before it is a result."
>
> Michelle Obama
> 1964 –
> lawyer, first lady, author

So, when a child is born by random destiny into a low achieving environment, one that lacks resources, guidance, and expectations ... that child's self-perception will likely reflect what they absorb.

When by that same unearned randomness, a child is born into a world of high expectations and support ... their mindset will reflect those as well. Being born into a Bush, Marsalis, or Manning home environment ... had clear impact on how those children developed.

expectations are goals

Expectations are game changers. They alter actions which change results and reinforce beliefs. They infuse our belief system ... shaping what seems possible.

Expectations are points of focus that cause our brains to look for solutions to fill in gaps. Our brains will find whatever it looks for, but it has to be asked to look. Expectations do just that.

15

people help shape our expectations

Maybe because we learn most from experience ... our perceptions of what's possible and acceptable are manipulated by those we hang around.

Dave, a close college teammate of mine recently passed away completely unexpected. At the service, his 19 year-old daughter Carly read a letter he had written to her when she began high school and was saved (by the school) to be read when she graduated. Carly is now a college freshman. In the letter Dave offered some loving comments and then 4 pieces of heartfelt fatherly advice. One of the last was ... "Remember we become who we spend time with. The quality of a person's life is most often a reflection of the expectations of their peer group. Choose your friends well."

"The quality of a person's life is most often a reflection of the expectations of their peer group. Choose your friends well."

Dave Whiteside
1958 – 2019
college teammate, lifelong friend

It was a moving letter to us all and though Dave did not knowingly predict an early departure ... it had the feel of last words to guide you when I'm gone, which come from deep in the heart.

Dave's life experience taught him that friendships matter immensely, that they help shape us and impact what we'll accomplish. I think he was saying find others who have been where you want to go and pay attention. Their attitudes and actions will point the way.

"There is nothing more critical to your success than the individuals you choose to surround yourself with."

George Raveling
1937 –
college basketball head coach

we learn from others instinctively

My daughter Kristin was about 9 months old and had been close to walking for some time, but had not taken her first step. One day 'Man-tuh' (Samantha) came over with her mom to visit. Samantha was a few months older and was walking anywhere she wanted. Kristin and Samantha spent the afternoon together with this now glaring gap.

Just after Samantha left, Kristin amazed Nancy and I. She clearly made a decision (as we found 9 month-olds can do). She decided it was her time to walk. She scooted down from Nancy's lap and was going to walk to me. She tried to stand up, but wobbled and fell. Got up, wobbled, and fell ... but started taking a step in between falls and inching closer towards me. With about 4 or 5 falls, she made it to me. We cheered and she was delighted. But no time for honors, she immediately turned to mommy determined to 'walk' back. She fell about 3 times, but never crawled. We cheered and she was again delighted with her small steps of success. With a couple more attempts, she finally walked the 8 feet with no falls, and her face was beaming.

I envision that Samantha's example had created both the expectation and the belief she needed. With a new belief that it was possible, she took the steps and learned from her mistakes until she got it.

we respond to what's expected of us

Just before my senior year in high school, our struggling basketball program hired a new coach, Ken Miller. He would go on to become one of the best ever in North Carolina with an 80% win percentage at the highest level and multiple state championships.

Prior to his arrival, our team culture was very contentious. It was not uncommon for practice to abruptly stop as players argued with the coach. We had teammates fighting on bus trips. During practice us smaller guys had to watch out for intentional elbows meant to harm. After practice my brother and I would leave immediately, as hanging around wasn't safe. Though our team was talented, we struggled to have winning seasons ... no surprise there.

Upon arrival, new head coach Miller immediately got to work changing the culture. First off, he let it be known that only sophomores could play JV (high school then was only $10^{th} - 12^{th}$). His new rule meant that juniors not quite ready for varsity and so playing JV, would get cut.

On hearing this, I commented to Coach Miller that some players would be really disappointed. His simple response has stayed with me over many years. He said with a little southern in his voice, "Well Bill, people respond to what's expected of them. They'll get used to it." I had no way of knowing how important that truth was going to be, but I soon saw it in action.

At the first practice, our best player (conference player of the year, to be) offered a little smack back to Coach Miller. Instantly and respectfully Coach responded, "You can leave now Shelt."

We all froze. Huh? ... What did we just hear? This is new talk. Has he just kicked our best player off the team for that?! Nobody moved.

Coach Miller repeated, "You can leave practice now Shelt. Come back tomorrow if you're ready to listen."

There was a pause that was only seconds but seemed much longer. Then Coach said, "Bye" and turned back to what he was teaching.

Shelt left angry, done for good I thought. And, just like that, everything was vastly different. We looked at each other wide-eyed, no words were needed. There was definitely a new sheriff in town. There were now new and very clear expectations. There were no favorites, and no bs was tolerated.

Coach Miller's expectations remained clear, high, and enforced. Guess who adjusted to whom? As we responded, we also saw that his way worked. In his first year, we won a very competitive Christmas tournament, went 17-5, and were co-champs in the toughest conference in the state. Along the way, we beat the preseason #11 team in the nation and the #3 team in our state. That was in just his first year.

Five years later he asked me to take his JV and Varsity to a team camp at East Carolina. He was now winning conference titles every year, had won a state title, and been runner up in another. His program reflected excellence and was well-respected across the state. 'Chapel Hill' on the jersey meant something. I remember how proud I was to be associated with Chapel Hill High basketball and Coach Miller.

> "People respond to what's expected of them."
>
> Coach Ken Miller
> 1942 –
> NC high school basketball coach

In hindsight I've realized that I got to witness the birth of a new culture and program, which all started with a change in expectations.

3 The Cause & Effect Spiral ©

Actions produce results, and thoughts produce actions. So now let's put these simple concepts in pictures and slap a name on it. The concepts are interconnected, fundamental to performance, and they determine whether we rise or fall in whatever is important to us. But other than that, they're useless.

The Cause & Effect Spiral ©

These concepts will soon form the basis for the AC Model. But for now, let's look at each factor independently to isolate key performance issues. We'll look at them in reverse order ... Results, then Actions, then Thoughts.

> "When you change what you believe, you change what you do... which changes what you get."
>
> Odille Rault
> author, speaker

20

Results

Results are simply outcomes, the effects of a cause. They are objective data without agenda or allegiance. They don't even have meaning until we attach some of our own.

Results are what we reap from the actions we have sown. While we get to choose our actions, what comes from them are simply responses ... and not something we control.

> "We are free to choose our actions, but we are not free to choose the consequences of these actions."
>
> Stephen Covey
> 1932 – 2012
> author, educator

Some results show up instantly and tangibly ... like the work of painters or carpenters. Other results can take weeks, months, or years to come to fruition ... like counseling, coaching, getting in shape, or changing a work culture.

> "The universe doesn't give you what you ask for with your thoughts; it gives you what you demand with your actions."
>
> Dr. Steve Maraboli
> 1975 –
> author, behavioral scientist

But regardless of how visible or invisible our actions (or inactions) are ... they still bring results, and those results accrue.

> "I saw that."
>
> Karma

results are perfect

A few years ago, I hired an IT student named Pat to come over to give our home an internet upgrade. An hour of work turned into a half day and multiple trips to the store, because things weren't working right.

As I grew more frustrated with the poorly performing wires and gadgets that it seemed were intentionally wreaking havoc on our day ... I became more and more impressed with how Pat patiently kept at it, methodically exploring different options. I eventually commented on his steady work and calm demeanor. I told him I admired his ability to keep an even keel when things weren't working right.

His response was something like this, "Well I learned something very valuable from a professor that really changed my perspective. This professor said that actually, things ALWAYS work perfectly. He said that we always get precisely the result the system is currently designed to produce. It is always doing its job just as it was told to do. Nothing more, nothing less. So if I don't like the result ... my job is to figure out the cause and change it."

What a profoundly simple and true concept ... that our results are not right or wrong. Rather they perfectly reflect what the current system is set up to produce. They are not mad at us. They are not inflicting some karma revenge. They are simply doing what they're told.

What if we acknowledged that truth in other aspects of our lives?

"Our life always expresses the result of our dominant thoughts."

Soren Kierkegaard
1813 – 1855
Danish philosopher, theologian, 'father of existentialism'

What about circumstances beyond our control?

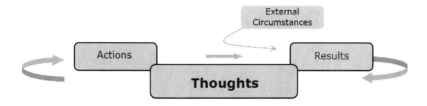

Certainly, events and circumstances beyond our control can and will alter on our lives. Where we regain control is in our ability to choose our response. No matter the damage caused, that ability remains.

A few years ago, a hurricane came through our city and the damage was extensive. We lost power for 10 days and our front porch became a camping gear kitchen and living room. All around, our community was buzzing with makeshift crews helping strangers clear debris. It seemed everyone participated in some way.

This external event created big change and the empathy was strong. But, at some point the hurricane card didn't have the same effect. It had a shelf life. If, months later, we rode by a house that had made zero progress cleaning up ... yet was capable of doing so ... it didn't illicit the same empathy as we did soon after the event.

It seems to me that we expect each other to become re-responsible when bad things occur. We can't be responsible for the hurricane, but we do intuitively expect each other to respond productively.

"You have power over your mind, not outside events. Realize this and you will find strength."

Marcus Aurelius
121 – 180 AD
Roman emperor, stoic philosopher

Actions are our observable behaviors … what we say and do.

We choose them, perform them, own them. Even inaction is observable and is an 'action' in terms of cause and effect.

Every day, we choose countless actions (or inactions) that each create micro-results. These micro-results stockpile, and over time create our reality.

Our actions reflect our beliefs, because we act based on what we believe to be our best option at the time. Even a person making the tragic decision to end their life … in that moment … has reduced their options and come to believe that suicide is their best remaining choice.

If you want to know who someone is, pay attention to their actions over time. We can fool some of the people some of the time… but eventually our outer world of actions and results syncs up with our inner thought world. We live what we believe.

"People may doubt what you say but they'll believe what you do."

Lewis Cass
1782 – 1866
military officer, politician

"Don't judge each day by the harvest you reap, but by the seeds you plant."

Robert Louis Stevenson
1850 – 1894
Scottish novelist

Thoughts

Our thoughts form us, in every way. It's impossible to over-state the role that our thoughts, our self-talk, has on who we are and what we become.

It's through our thoughts that we make sense of and interact with our world.

> "All that we are is the result of what we have thought."
>
> Siddhartha Gautama
> ~563 BC – 483 BC
> philosopher, teacher, founder of Buddhism

Our thoughts drive our emotions, our decisions, our actions. They determine how we interact with the world around us, which in turn shapes our world.

Within our thought world … is our story about ourselves, which we hold as certainty. But actually, it's only a story that includes a mix of truths, part truths, and untruths. Nevertheless, we act in accordance with that story, both consciously and subconsciously. Then in circular logic, when our results are consistent with our actions … we use that to verify our initial story. In reality, our results are only verifying our actions. We'll talk more about that regarding self-fulfilling prophecies.

The main point is, our thoughts and perceptions and stories are powerful.

> "We do not see things as they are, we see things as we are."
>
> The Talmud, a collection of ancient Jewish writings

data gets interpreted

Data comes at us all day every day, and without intrinsic meaning. It is simply data, the effects of some cause.

It's our brain's job to create some kind of order and meaning from all that we perceive so we can function in the world.

> "We don't succeed or fail, we get results."
>
> Tony Robbins
> 1960 –
> author, speaker

"Niekas neturi prasmės, išskyrus tai, ką mes pridedame prie jo."

That string of letters means absolutely nothing to me. But to a Lithuanian it means something like: "Nothing has meaning except what we attach to it." We see the very same characters. The difference is not in the data, but in the meaning we attach to it.

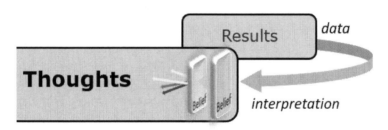

Established beliefs are our lenses that help interpret data. Because we do not all have the same established beliefs or understandings ... we 'see' things differently.

If I come to believe (tell myself), "I'm not worthy of love" then data will get interpreted through that lens. When someone treats me poorly, or something goes wrong... that experience will filter through my 'I'm unworthy' lens. It will unfairly slant my interpretation.

My perception of events, and thus my emotions, and my decisions will be altered by my personal interpretation ... and it all may be based on illusionary truth.

our interpretations are fallible

We reach our conclusions based on our unique set of experiences and influences. It seems the more biased we are, the less aware we are of where they came from and their influence over us. Misinterpretations can be costly.

A sobering example is now well documented in *When They See Us* ... a true story docuseries on the 5 black teenagers (Central Park Five) who were accused of raping and beating a jogger in 1989. They were convicted, imprisoned, but then exonerated in 2002.

> "We can't depend on our eyes when our imagination is out of focus."
>
> Mark Twain
> 1835 – 1910
> writer, humorist

The series shows precisely where authorities made grossly biased decisions in opposition to physical evidence. To fit their established beliefs, authorities illegally coerced guilty pleas from innocent and frightened teenagers. The media took the bait and rushed to judgement. Even private citizens unassociated with the facts, campaigned for their own biased verdict ... that young black kids must certainly be guilty.

Even the title *When They See Us*, gets to the idea that we see through a lens. In this case ... contaminated lenses, not evidence, convicted these five young men. Overnight, they went from their caring families and school activities to the hell of an adult prison. Twelve years later the real assailant came forward and previously disregarded DNA evidence confirmed their innocence. *prejudice*

The point is, established beliefs (lenses) are how we see the world. And they can powerfully distort any scene with our shortcomings. They fool us, and they make fools of us. Fighting for objectivity is a lifelong challenge.

how I became my family's big dog wimp

When I was 6, our neighborhood had two ominous dogs. One was a chained-up Chow named Tycene, who snarled at anything that came near it. The other was his German Shepard sidekick.

Two or three times a year Tycene would break his chain, scale his 6-foot fence, and then go on a rampage seeking revenge on the free world. His German Shepard buddy would hear his bugle and join in.

Our beautiful day in the neighborhood instantly became a war zone. With adults screaming, "Get in the house!" it felt like we were running for our lives. Equally frightening was that our family beagle, Wags ... stirred by his best instincts and worst logic ... would rush headlong into harm's way to tangle with these vicious attack dogs. We were certain he'd never make it back.

Like the rest of us, good ole Wags did survive. When we moved away, he carried a nicely split left ear courtesy of Tycene ... which for the rest of his dog days we saw as a badge of courage.

My primary take away was less glamorous ... I retained a strong belief that big dogs want to chew me up.

> "You can't control everything that happens to you, but you can decide what it means."
>
> Raeb

man or mouse?

Fast forward a generation and I'm walking with my 8-year-old daughter Kristin. We come upon a big dog which still signals to me ... danger! I start looking for a way for us to escape.

But she, raised in less dog turbulent times, doesn't flinch and is eager to make friends with this enemy. I'm tentative, then surprised that they always love her ... I don't get it.

Epilogue: My big dog misbeliefs were challenged when my now adult daughter Kristin got a 70 lb pit bull. It took 50 years, but I discovered that Koco, and many of her friends, are ferociously lovable.

My Tycene take-aways are things like: my perception is my reality ... we learn best from our own experience ... telling isn't teaching.

You can tell me all day that big dogs are kind and loving, but I learned through experience they were mean, and I only unlearned that through experience with Koco.

first-hand experience

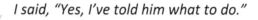

Telling isn't teaching, listening isn't learning.

Years ago, as a new instructor on high ropes course activities, I was teaching participants to belay their partners. I had given directions to the lead belayer (2 backing him up) when my mentor, Michael Stein, asked me if this belayer was ready.

I said, "Yes, I've told him what to do."

Michael's question back to me became a light bulb moment. He said, "Yes, I heard what you told him, but do his HANDS know what to do?"

Hmmm, good question. Michael was saying that just because he had heard it, does not mean he can do it. Head knowledge and body knowledge are not the same thing ... there's a translation process between them that requires activity, experience.

That comment shed light on an important truth about coaching. Though I knew intuitively that 'telling isn't teaching' and though experience had always been my primary teacher in life ... I was still overly impressed with my words.

His hands needed to tell him he was ready ... not me and not even him ... but his own experience.

"Tell me and I forget. Teach men and I remember. Involve me and I learn."

Benjamin Franklin
1706 – 1790
statesman, writer

the C&E Spiral implies momentum

The Cause & Effect Spiral© is a visual of the transfer of energy between Thoughts and Actions and Results. But after a cycle, what happens with that energy? Does it dissipate without effect?

My vision is that each cycle influences the next toward sameness. If a cycle has negative energy, its influence on the next is negative, just as a positive cycle would have a positive influence on the next. This momentum works in directions … moving upward or downward, expanding or contracting, getting lighter or heavier.

Upward movement is good, downward movement not so good and needs change. But change is hard, and thus good coaching is valuable.

upward momentum example

Thoughts … "Ok, I can try this for one week. It won't kill me."
Actions … I cut grains, dairy, and added sugar from my diet for a week.
Results … I notice more energy and a lighter feel.
Thoughts … "I love the better feel. My diet is quite acceptable even without these foods. I must be helping my cardio vascular system. I can do this another week."

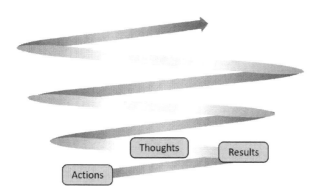

downward momentum example

Thoughts … "I really doubt it'll make much difference, and taking things out of my diet will be so painful. I'll miss so much if I do that."

Actions … I make an attempt at diet changes, but on day 3, I give in to old habits. That semi attempt continues all week.
Results … No changes are noticeable.
Thoughts … "I knew I couldn't lose weight."

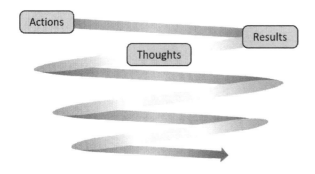

shifting momentum upward

The important question is how do we shift a downward spiral into an upward one? The short answer is … with small steps that build positive momentum.

Negative spirals can have years of habit on their side. They won't be overcome instantly. You don't get in shape in a day, or master the guitar in a day. But you can take doable action steps in a day and they have impact too. As a matter of fact, that's all you can do.

The upcoming Part 2 will get into how to make small adjustments at various points on the spiral … any of which will contribute to an upward shift and the beginning of positive momentum.

Part
2

Shifting Momentum Upward
getting unstuck

In AC terminology, coaching is about helping others shift downward spirals into upward ones. But where and how?

This section gets into specific practices that will impact a downward trending spiral.

I consider this section a supplement to the AC coaching strategies that will come in Part 4. Yet the concepts are completely consistent.

4 The Magic of Thinking Small

My friend James Lloyd is from NC but lives in CA. For years now we've talked a few times each week. Both challenges and encouragement come easy and often between us. It's a valuable friendship.

In younger days James was an excellent football player at Wake Forest University, known for his tenacity and passion. Among many enduring tales is the one that caused him to be carried off the field after a kick off against NC State. James' job was to take out one of the three blockers in the wedge (those right in front of the ball carrier). But in kamikaze fashion, James decide to take out all 3 blockers by diving and laying himself out horizontally in midair. The collision worked and he was knocked unconscious. So that's a bit about James.

Like with many ex-athletes, he later got out of shape. No male in his family had lived past 63 and he was approaching that milestone with no expectation of being the first.

As he moved through his fifties, his weight was going up and his health was spiraling downward. He was diabetic, had lost all feeling in the front of his feet, was told that major back surgery was looming, and was on 13 medications. A walk to the mailbox was a challenge.

On one of our talks, James lamented that he missed getting outside and enjoying a good walk. Remembering my Uncle Bill's quote below I encouraged him to just do what he could ... even if just to walk up the street one mailbox. I thought he would decline, but he tried it ... then later that day walked it again.

We talked the next day, it was obvious he had shifted.

> "Take one day at a time and do the best you can with what you've got."
>
> my Great Uncle Will Rhea Winfrey
> 1916 – 2012
> football star, WWII vet, Army colonel, blind his last 50 years

The next few days he continued ... walking a house, then two, then three ... seeing bits of progress. Then, he did what was unthinkable just a week before ... he walked up and out of his cul-de-sac which meant going uphill about 10 houses. It was a major accomplishment for someone who felt so immobile just days ago.

Those ventures outside turned into walks, and the momentum has grown to the point that James has walked at least 5 miles every day for over 2 years now. It's astonishing. In that time, he's walked over 6 thousand miles, taken over 4 million steps. He just walked 300 miles in one month (10/day), and has hiked on Mt Whitney and in Death Valley.

The results of his actions are life changing. With his new walking routines and a sensible diet ... he's down 100 lbs and is off of every medication, including insulin. He recently had a medical worker marvel at the very good circulation in his feet, despite having no feeling. In addition to the physical benefits, he considers walking to be his anti-depressant.

James is a hero. Those are big accomplishments. He gives me some credit ... but all I did was suggest a small step. The power surge came with his decision to act, to take small steps that built momentum. He woke up his superpower.

Successful people are not ones without setbacks or failures or stagnation or discouragements. They are rather ones that have figured ways to turn things around.

So how do we turn a downward spiral upward? The best answer I've ever found is ... with small doable steps that spark momentum.

When mountain top goals demotivate ... it's time to find smaller, more doable goals. And no matter the bigger goal, the new goal is now to simply create some positive movement. Even the smallest steps have great potential to do so. Just as a wood stove that ends up heating the whole room starts small ... so our small steps have great ability because of the momentum they can generate.

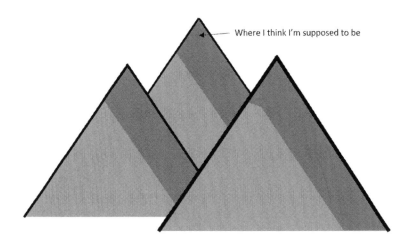

Where I think I'm supposed to be

Where I think I am

all we are saying ... is give momentum a chance

We gain the benefit of movement not because we understand it, but because we engage it. It has its own innate ability to create change. A few examples come instantly to mind.

Dave Ramsey's financial seminars advise people to tackle smallest debts first, no matter the interest rate. He wants you to see progress and build motivation. He's after momentum.

> "Momentum begets momentum, and the best way to start is to start."
>
> Gil Penchina
> 1969 –
> American business executive

A childhood friend of mine, Lenny, shared some good advice he got from his father, Henry Anderson, a well-respected community leader. His dad said, "Whenever you're discouraged or depressed ... go clean something. Anything, even one drawer." The point was just be productive, even in small amounts. Then watch how it shifts your outlook. He was using the power of momentum.

In another era of my life, I ran every day, usually the same 3-mile hilly course that I ran pretty hard. If I went to bed without running ... I'd lay there feeling bad and thinking about getting back up. But 3 miles was too much, I didn't have the energy. I found though, that I could trick myself. I make a small goal of just going a block ... one easy block ... and then I'd keep my streak intact. So, I'd get up and get out the door. Without fail, I always ran farther than that one block. Usually I'd end up on a very good 3-mile run. I'm not sure what it says about me that I was able to trick myself over and over.

> "Action will destroy your procrastination."
>
> Og Mandino
> 1923 – 1996
> author, speaker

The next 4 chapters will look at 4 points on the spiral where small shifts can turn momentum upward. They areas to pay close attention to when coaching others or ourselves.

- Results – *clarify what and why*
- Actions – *find doable steps*
- Emotions – *learn from reactions*
- Beliefs – *tell yourself a better truth*

Then, the last chapter in Part 2 is about a simple 5-minute technique to initiate small change … Raeb Mapping.

"You become successful the moment you start moving towards a worthwhile goal."

Samuel Johnson
1709 – 1784
English writer

"If I cannot do great things, I can do small things in a great way."

Dr. Martin Luther King, Jr
1929 – 1968
minister, social change leader

"Courage doesn't always roar. Sometimes courage is the quiet voice at the end of the day saying, 'I will try again tomorrow'."

Mary Ann Radmacher
1957 –
writer, artist

5 Results
clarify what and why

This chapter says Results, but it's really about motivation. That's because … the degree results matter determines the energy we'll expend. Results by themselves are just cold data. It's the value we place on them that creates energy.

Consider the difference between you cleaning your house because someone told you to, versus cleaning your house because you have special company coming soon who has never seen your place. Those two scenarios are the exact same task, but are not attacked with the same energy and attention to detail. The difference is motivation.

Motivation is magical energy, and everything needs energy. If you've ever been sick enough to experience energy depletion … you come away with a new perspective of the importance of energy. It made me consider what life is without energy. It's not really much life.

Motivation produces energy. Time spent fostering motivation is time well spent.

It's hard to imagine the energy it took to build the pyramids. The Giza Pyramid took 20 years to build and was the tallest man-made structure for the next 4,000 years. Where in the world did the energy come from to accomplish such a task? ... to force 100k slaves into such labor all those years? ... to work through so many obstacles? ... to endure untold toil and sweat and suffering and death? Why?

Their mammoth energy came from some compelling reason. Whatever it was, that reason mattered enough to power enormous efforts.

Slaves of course were cruelly forced, moved by the whip and their strong will to survive. Those unforced ... who chose to be cruel, to spend such vast national resources had other reasons. Their reasons may have been fabricated illusionary truths ... but they produced boundless energy nevertheless.

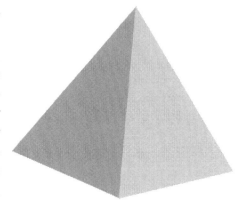

It's not possible to imagine sustained significant effort without legit motivation. We don't do things very long just because. Results and motivation are interrelated.

other thoughts

energy is like money

Most of us have a limited amount of both and should use them wisely. We can invest them in ways that build more, or spend them in ways that deplete without return.

spend energy to get energy

Hard work is tiring, but bad hard work depletes us sooner and more completely because we lose motivation. Work that has little value, is majoring in the minors, or not being effective ... is a battery drain. But hard work that is focused effort towards meaningful goals is a battery recharge even if we're physically exhausted.

What's deceptive is that tiredness from either feels similar, and the instincts are to take a break. For good work, the break is a fix and we'll come back stronger. For bad work, not so much. The best fix here is to find good work ... find what's more valuable to us... and then make a few small steps of progress on that. It'll take energy we feel we don't have, but energy invested in good work returns with 'interest'.

Satisfaction = expectation – results

We can only be frustrated about something we want and expect. If we don't care, or never expected it ... it's a non-issue. But when we want and expect it, yet can't get it ... that's frustrating.

It could be that our expectations are unrealistic. Or ... they could be reasonable but our actions are to blame. Examine both objectively.

> Expectation is the mother of frustration.

Unmotivated people may be among the most motivated

Some who appear unmotivated may instead be hurt or discouraged, precisely because of their strong motivation. A strong drive to achieve with poor results can look a lot like lack of motivation. When coaching someone who has become unmotivated, explore this possibility. There may be a fix that is simpler than you think.

we're motivated by things we do well

It's encouraging to be good at something. Sometimes we begin to like something simply because we do it well. It's not a guarantee that we'll like it, but it sure can help.

> "Nothing succeeds like success."
>
> my mom *(a saying from her childhood)*

Certainly, the opposite is true. Not doing something well can take the joy out of the task, as we lose hope that we can get it right. So, as a coach, when you help someone do a task well, chances are you're increasing motivation as well.

we are all experts in something … find one valuable to others

Our brain figures out anything we do over and over. But to make a living, or a contribution… the question is, how valuable is my expertise to others? If it is valued that's good. If it is both valued and unique … then you've really got something.

The fact that developing your expertise feels difficult may be the very reason to keep going. If it was easy, everyone would be an expert and your uniqueness and value would drop.

there is such a thing as self-induced depression

Our negative emotions, lasting sour moods, or enduring depression can be partially or fully the result of our choices.

It's a deep subject and this is only the shallow end. But the point is that we often overlook how much our emotional state is affected by things we have control over ... our thoughts, actions, and results.

When our actions and results lack value ... it has a draining effect. In those situations, our spirit is living on junk food, being malnourished.

Spending lots of time and effort on things of little value to us ... is depleting. But when we see results in meaningful pursuits ... like maybe getting to the gym, or completing a home project, or doing an important task at work well ... it brightens our outlook. It changes our confidence and motivation.

"Actions are the anti-
dote to despair."

Joan Baez
1941 –
singer, song writer

"Where there is hope, there's life. It fills us with fresh courage and makes us strong again."

Anne Frank
1929 – 1944
German / Dutch diarist, holocaust victim

The power of inspiration comes from what we value. To gain some clarity on what we are doing and why, consider these questions:

at work
- How does my role contribute to team & company goals?
- What expectations do others have of my role?
- Which tasks within my role are most important?
- Who might be an asset in helping me do my role better?

an undone project
- How will completion feel?
- What will be newly possible once completed?
- How will this impact others around me?
- What small step can I take now?

personal passions
- What problem in the world would I love to fix?
- What have been the reoccurring themes in my work life?
- What do others say I am passionate about?
- What successes have made me feel the most confident?
- What things do I get immersed in, lose track of time?

future work
- What would I do for no pay?
- What skills come naturally to me?
- What do others seek input from me on?
- What 3 things did I enjoy doing today or this week?
- How can I do them for pay?

6 Actions
find doable steps

We can't always do great things, but we can always do something.

Even if our get up and go, done got up and went (mentioned in honor of my dad, who liked that saying) … there always remains SOMETHING we are capable of doing. Small steps are extremely valuable because of the innate power of movement and momentum.

Let's look at a technique that generates movement. It's not a pill … so it will require a bit of effort. But it's useful anytime you feel a certain you or a project is stuck and needs a boost. Follow these two steps:

First … find a 'doable' action.

Propose progressively smaller actions until your gut acknowledges, "Ok, I can do that." That is your move. No matter how stuck you are, there is always a move you can make. Just find it.

The goal isn't big action, it's just action … any action. So, it can be as small as it needs to be … just one pointed in a positive direction.

"Courage is only the accumulation of small steps."

Gyorgy Konrad
1933 – 2019
Hungarian novelist, advocate for individual freedom

47

In those moments, finding a doable action is like looking for a spot where the creek narrows enough that you sense you can make the jump. You consider one spot but, no … it's too far. You keep walking and when we see it, you know it in your gut you can make that jump.

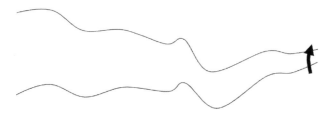

Second … 1,2,3 jump!

Now it's time to act. No more thought, just act. No need for a great feeling … you just do it. You count to yourself … 1,2,3, then jump! No feelings, no reasoning … just action. Take the step. You won't die.

The good thing is, we gain the benefit of action whether we understand how it works or not. Movement generates benefits externally in the form of results or micro-results … and internally as it shifts our perspective and our confidence.

Suggestion … try this right now on something small that you've been putting off. Just do it. An email, a small home task, anything … just find a small doable action and then … 1,2,3 jump!

Action!

"Stay afraid, but do it anyway, what's important is the action. You don't have to wait to be confident. Just do it and eventually confidence will follow."

Carrie Fisher
1956 –
actress, writer

"But those Woulda-Coulda-Shouldas all ran away and hid from one little Did."

Shel Silverstein
1930 – 1999
writer

my friend and mentor, Dick DeVenzio

As an aspiring young basketball player, I hit the lottery early on. At age 11, I met Dick DeVenzio who became a very impressionable mentor and later a lifelong friend. From age 14 until 23, I spent summers working his camps … learning from one of the top innovators of any sport.

Late in that run, at an invitational camp and in front of 100 of the best high school players on the east coast … I was beside him when he issued a challenge to a specific player. He wanted to motivate this guy to be persistent in his training. Dick said, "If you'll do [whatever] for 20 minutes every day, I promise you this time next year you'll have conquered your weakness. I promise!"

He then paused, as if enlightened, and turned the challenge back towards himself. He said with resolve, to the whole group … "As a matter of fact, I'll do that with you this year. I've got an instructional basketball book I've been meaning to write but have not gotten done. So, I'm committing to all of you all right here that I will write one page a day … and I'll have a book here this time next year."

Dick returned to camp the next year with a published book called "Stuff Good Players Should Know" which has since become a classic in the basketball world.

That day, I watched Dick engage his super power of small doable steps.

> "You'll never change your life until you change something you do daily. The secret to success is found in your daily routine"
>
> John Maxwell
> 1947 –
> author, speaker, pastor

basketball in the late middle ages

A few years ago I was way out of basketball shape. I hadn't tried to compete with the good high school / college age players in 4 years.

I began going back to the Y just for exercise, playing was nowhere on the horizon. I noticed a guy a few years older than me and more out of shape than me with a good stretching routine. I quietly started copying what he was doing.

About three weeks later, my body was feeling much different and my thoughts were shifting too. I heard thoughts like ... "Hey you, why not give it a try?!" and, "You just might be able to play again."

I soon lowered my expectations and stepped on the court with two simple goals ... get exercise and don't get hurt. The first day I was quite rusty skill-wise and so very winded ... but I accomplished my only goals. I left encouraged to take another step. Soon I was playing 2 to 3 days per week. Awkwardness was leaving and familiarity was returning. In a few months, my body felt good and my ability to compete had risen. It was quite fun. That comeback (#8?) lasted about 3 years and during that time I played better than I had in 25 years. To me it was a mountain top accomplishment, something I thought had long passed me by.

But what got me going was not a mountain top expectation, that was way too far away. Rather, it was the small steps of that stretching routine that generated momentum.

"Sometimes, the most radical thing we can be is consistent."

Mitch Mitchell
friend, minister

"Inspiration does exist, but it must find you working."

Pablo Picasso
1881 – 1973
Spanish painter, sculptor

some doable steps

Maybe it's focusing on 1 good diet day, or one healthy meal … instead of a 7 day fast. Or going for a 1 block jog … instead of a tough 3-mile weighted vest run. Or getting yourself to the gym for the sauna … instead of for a difficult workout. Maybe it's getting 1 page written … instead of expecting a well-organized chapter. Maybe it's not committing to mowing the whole yard now … but saying I can at least go get the mower out. Maybe it's not cleaning the whole kitchen now … it's just getting a few things soaking in water.

The point is, it's taking one step now, generating movement in the right direction. The goal is not the mountain top, it's movement.

I recently read a social media post on this subject that said, "Start by doing 1 push up, by drinking 1 cup of water, by paying toward 1 debt, by reading 1 page, by making 1 sale, by deleting 1 old contact, by walking 1 lap, by attending 1 event, by writing 1 paragraph. Start today. Repeat tomorrow."

The idea that many others have recognized is, just take the next doable step, then repeat.

"If you hear the dogs, keep going. If you see the torches, keep going. If there's shouting after you, keep going. Don't ever stop. Keep going. If you want to taste freedom, keep going."

Harriet Tubman
1820 – 1913
American abolitionist, led 13 missions on the Underground Railroad that freed over 70 slaves

you don't have to feel it to do it

Inspiration is great, but results don't care how you felt. We gain the benefit of a walk or washing clothes whether or not we were inspired beforehand.

actions change moods

Our moods and actions are connected. Taking care of important matters has a positive impact on our psyche, just as neglecting them has a negative one. We feel bad when we're neglecting responsibilities. Sometimes, the real challenge is to find what we've neglected that is causing a sour mood.

> "Happiness is not something ready-made. It comes from your own actions."
>
> Dalai Lama
> 1935 –
> spiritual leader of Tibet

once unstuck not always unstuck

Getting unstuck is not a one and done proposition, it's an ongoing process. Don't think you're the oddball because you feel like you're constantly looking for small steps to get you going again.

commit to small chunks of time

One way to break procrastination ... is to make your small step an amount of time. Example: 'I'll clean-up for 10 minutes.' Or, 'I'll read for 15 minutes.' Make the amount of time non-intimidating.

create a clear path of doable steps

On complex projects, create clear steps with due dates. List them out and track progress. Clear next steps enable you to focus on small action steps, which build momentum. actions.

start with the easy steps first

When a project is dragging, but you have a list of steps ... forget the order and pick a step that you can complete easily, and repeat. When you hit the tougher tasks, you'll have more momentum on your side.

find what's bugging you

When you have an 'unexplained' energy drop, not just tired and in need of a good night's rest, but lacking moti- vation ... look for a cause.

Unresolved issues and undone projects sap energy. Sometimes the hardest part is finding the origin of the frustration. It takes honest reflection and then action to fix them.

column 1: Make a list of 5 things that need your attention.

column 2: Rate the urgency of each task (1-5)

column 3: Rate the amount of pain felt if left undone (1-5)

(5 = a lot, 1 = a little)

Now, use that feedback to pick 1 on your list to act on immediately. Take a minute to imagine it completed, and how that would feel. Then, initiate a doable step.

> "Start where you are. Use what you have. Do what you can."
>
> Arthur Ashe
> 1943 – 1993
> American tennis professional

choose to versus have to

A friend on social media recently said his goal at work was to never be asked a second time to do something … never. He wants to move himself, not be moved.

choose to: is acting from our own decision, without prodding. It's starting our own engine.

have to: is being prodded into action by deadlines, peer pressure, or others, and not our own initiative.

"My guiding philosophy is 'choice not chance'. I teach young people they can make choices every day that give them control over their lives. My calling is to empower others, and I choose to do it through basketball."

Joanne McCallie
1965 –
Duke women's basketball, head coach

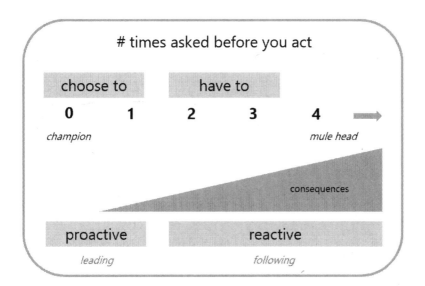

"Oh crap, that's due tomorrow?!" Thomas Jefferson, July 3, 1776

A recent Facebook post I made as a tribute to my friend Wayman, maybe the most impressive 'choose to' guy I've ever known.

The Y family lost a good man this past week, Wayman Hines. One of the most dependable, hard-working men I've ever met.

He was in charge of the facility for two decades and did an excellent job. Wayman would arrive about 1 am every day to get work done before his staff arrived about 5 am to open the place up. He'd stay until late morning and then go to a second job, not because he had to but because of his work ethic. For years he cared for his ailing wife until she passed away a year ago.

He once told me that he never wanted to have to be told what to do, so he went and found whatever needed to be done and did it before anyone asked.

Wayman would allow himself to play ball with us one morning a week... always on Fridays. He was a feisty player and a good friend to us all. He took special care of the morning basketball group. For example, he made sure we always had our own high-quality basketballs (out of his budget) that he kept hidden in his office so they wouldn't get stolen or worn down by others. And he gave us the red-carpet privilege of being able to get them out of his office any time of day.

Wayman was a very good man and he left a great example ... worthy of respect.

Picture: Wayman was voted by staff and members to be the first person to go down the Y's new water slide. This picture is him as he waves to the crowd.

7 Emotions
learn from reactions

life without emotion?

emotions and thoughts

We don't grow without changing our thinking. Much of what makes change difficult is being unaware of the thoughts steering us. Up to 95% of our thought process is considered non-conscious. That percentage includes autonomic responses like heart and lungs, but still leaves room for a good chunk of discretionary thoughts that bypass our attention. We all have a lot to discover within our thought world.

One way to become more aware of our hidden thoughts is through our emotions. Emotions are an excellent informant because they're linked to thoughts and beliefs. As we become more observant of emotions, we can become more aware of stealthy thoughts. That's what this chapter is about.

emotions give life flavor

Imagine your favorite dinner with special people. The food comes and everyone is raving over it. But you, unfortunately, do not have the ability to taste. The company is great, but the food is like tasteless grits. What a difference taste makes. And just maybe, as taste is to a meal, so emotions are to our lives.

the absence of emotion

What if ... you win a hard-fought championship game, yet feel nothing. Or you buy the house we've always wanted, but without emotion. Or, your child is born, or you lose a family member to cancer, but can only calculate these changes in terms of needs and tasks. Life without emotions would be nothing like we can live today. Emotions are how we taste life. All the more reason to understand and manage them well.

emotions are energy moving through the body

There is no scientific consensus on what an emotion is, but let's start with the original Latin word, *emotere,* which literally means ... energy in motion. So, think of emotions as energy moving through the body. That energy can be positive or negative, upward or downward, expanding (joy, happiness) or contracting (fear, resentment).

emotions are reactive

"Feelings follow thought."

Raeb

Emotions merge the mental and physical. Amazingly, we think something and experience a physical response. Ideally, that response helps us (fight or flight). But they can also impair our thinking and ability to respond ... another reason to better manage emotions.

emotions imprint

"Memories are tricky. We remember how it felt, not necessarily how it was."

James Taylor
1948 –
singer, songwriter

Events are imprinted through the emotions we experience. We remember where we were on 9/11 type events due to intense emotions. We remember people or things from our childhood that others don't because of how they made us feel. Emotions leave an impression.

Emotions are largely in reaction to our beliefs … our perception of reality. They don't materialize randomly or from celestial alignment.

If I believe a monster is under my bed, I'll be scared … monster or no monster. If a person with dementia believes someone is breaking into their room, their emotions will be very real even though the thieves are not. People have been informed that they won the lottery, then later told it was a mistake. Their initial joy was natural, but was based on belief and not reality.

The reverse is also true. If I am actually in danger but unaware … I'll have no fear emotion. If I've been chosen for a promotion but have yet to be told, there's no emotion. We feel based on what we perceive, not on reality. As our thoughts change, our feelings change.

This more detailed version of the C&E Spiral© reflects feelings following thought. Data is presented, we interpret data (mind) and a thought or perception is generated. Emotion is a reaction to that thought. Then we choose a response … led by some combination of emotion and reason.

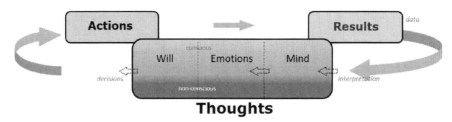

Thoughts

The Cause & Effect Spiral©

emotions are information

This may be the most important feature about emotions as it relates to Adaptive Coaching.

Because emotions are connected to thoughts, they're like a fisherman's pot buoy saying ... "Look under here." As we identify emotions ... we can then explore to find their triggering beliefs. Because beliefs can be well hidden, emotions are valuable information.

emotions are arrogant

 They come across like they know everything, like they are absolutely right, no questions asked. But the fact is they have no intellect about them. They only do what they are told to do. They do not think things through. They just take a thought and run with it. They're too arrogant to reason with.

emotions are gullible

You can tell them anything and they'll believe it instantly ... even fly off the handle without legit proof. They're like the person who sees bizarre made-up news from the internet fringes and immediately blasts it out as absolute truth. Like those easily stirred folks, reasoning is not the job of emotion.

> "Never say never, because limits, like fears are often just an illusion."
>
> Michael Jordan
> 1963 –
> NBA player, owner

emotions and moods

And let's make a simple distinction between emotions and moods:

Emotions are an immediate response to a known stimulus (ex: a bad call by the referee, a good grade in school).

Moods are longer lasting emotional states where we often are not so aware of the underlying cause.

some tendencies:

Emotions	Moods
• lasts seconds or minutes	• can last hours, days, weeks, or years
• have a specific trigger event	• a less clear trigger
• numerous specific emotions: mad, sad, glad, embarrassed, afraid … plus variations	• 2 main feelings: positive and negative
• more outwardly observable	• less outwardly observable
• overt, reactionary	• covert, enduring

managing emotions

emotions influence

Especially as leaders, we influence people in both overt and covert ways. Communication is not confined to our well thought-out talking points. Rather, we are ALWAYS communicating. People are constantly receiving and perceiving 'messages' from us, whether we know it or not.

> "You cannot not communicate."
>
> Paul Watzlawick
> 1921 – 2007
> Austrian / American family therapist, psychologist

Our communication is not just what we say ... or what we think we say. Rather it's what others interpret ... from what they hear, see, and feel from us. We're told that over 90% of communication is non-verbal. Scripted speeches do not override the messages we send with our whole self. Our actions and demeanor ... will speak loudly.

The point here is that emotions communicate and influence strongly. If my emotions convey fear, stress, anger, distrust, delight, joy ... that will dominate the messages I send out.

> "I no longer listen to what people say. I just watch what they do. Behavior never lies."
>
> Winston Churchill
> 1874 – 1965
> British Prime Minister, writer

Understanding and managing emotions is important because of the magnified influence leaders have on others ... and because of the significant role emotional maturity plays in development.

Let's look at 3 aspects of managing emotions:

1. **recognize**
2. **express**
3. **control**

1 recognizing emotions

A basic of self-awareness is being able to identify the emotions and moods we're feeling. Let's look at them in more detail.

In this book we'll use the term emotion more than moods. While there are differences between these two (often shades of grey), healthy responses to each are similar.

5 categories of emotions

To begin to recognize an emotion, start by finding the category it most closely connects to:

- *Mad* ... someone or something has been wronged
- *Sad* ... a loss of something of value
- *Glad* ... the presence of something of value
- *Embarrassed* ... falling short of expectations
- *Afraid* ... feeling threatened

emotions and intensity

5 Continuums of Emotion©

	Bothered	Disappointed	Satisfied	Shy	Cautious
less	Frustrated	Discouraged	Pleased	Self-conscious	Anxious
	Mad	**Sad**	**Glad**	**Embar-rassed**	**Afraid**
	Angry	Depressed	Excited	Ashamed	Terrified
more	Furious	Despondent	Elated	Humiliated	Panicked

You'll find charts that have more or fewer core emotions and with other descriptive words that would fit as well. This is just my overview.

In any particular situation, more than one emotion can be at play. For example, I can be both mad and sad that my car was wrecked.

emotions are universal

No matter how much difference or distance exists between two individuals ... oceans, languages, time periods, status, culture, age, race ... we all united in our shared emotions.

We don't all have the same goals ... but we all know what success and failure feel like. We have not all lost the same thing ... but we all know the pain of grief. We do not all value the same things ... but we all know what love and sacrifice feel like. Our common humanity is prevalent and prominent ... far greater than our differences.

find beliefs that trigger your emotions

- *Mad*: What <u>wrong</u> bothers me?

- *Sad*: What <u>loss</u> could I be feeling?

- *Glad*: What am I <u>pleased</u> with?

- *Embarrassed*: What of me (or us) is <u>subpar</u>?

- *Afraid*: What is <u>threatening</u>?

2 expressing emotions

not speaking up

While it's important to be able put preferences aside to blend well with others ... an overuse of that is unhealthy.

Neglecting your own ideas and emotions is also exhausting. The more we disregard our emotions, the more our inner and outer self are incongruent. That's called emotional dissonance, which takes extra energy to maintain and can lead to burnout.

When emotions go unidentified or unexpressed, they don't just go away. They hide, they fester, and eventually ignite. They can either explode or implode.

An explosion is when the external response doesn't match the situation. A small match ignites compressed (unspoken) emotions. The exaggerated response means that collateral damage is likely. For example, a coworker has a pattern of cutting corners that goes undiscussed, until one more small detail is left out which leads to a blowup reaction and damaging comments.

An implosion is when the negative reaction is turned inward and affects the individual who blames or criticizes themselves. For example, if my role on the team is being under-valued and I don't speak up ... that compressed frustration lead to lose of confidence, growing discouragement, or even depression.

speaking up

It's good to let yourself be heard in the world you live in. How, when, and to whom we express does matter ... but suppression is not a good long-term solution. use "I" statements I feel in,

We gain from our exercise of speaking up regardless of the listener's response. Their response belongs to them. Regardless of how another receives it, the process we go through to put feelings into words, to say them out loud, and to then witness a response ... can change our perspective and spark momentum.

4 Steps to Constructive Conversations: (a separate Adaptive Team Leadership workshop)

Go, Ask, Tell, Find I's

> "There is no greater agony than bearing an untold story inside you."
>
> Maya Angelo
> 1928 – 2014
> poet, writer

Go to the Source ... don't complain to those who can't fix the issue ... get to the source of your conflict and initiate the conversation

Ask to Learn ... don't listen to oppose or to win an argument, instead ask good questions and listen to understand their perspective

Tell Your Story ... speak your mind with both truth and respect ... be clear about impacts on yourself or others ... be heard

Find Common High Ground ... be willing to give some ... know what you can and cannot lose ... find what's common ... clarify decisions

to get something off your chest

If your words are both respectful and truthful, you'll be amazed at what you can say that you thought you never could. With those two qualities, you'll be willing to say more, and they'll be willing to hear more. So be both respectful and truthful ... and share:

- *the emotion* ... what you feel and its intensity (see 5 continuums of emotion earlier in this chapter)

- *the root cause* ... the beliefs or perspectives connected to the emotions (the wrong that makes you mad, the loss that makes you sad, what you're glad about, what's embarrassing, what makes you afraid)

- *the impact* ... how you or others are affected by the situation

To decrease tension ... put the emphasis on how YOU are being impacted, instead on them and how they behaved as a bad guy. That subtle shift can mean a lot. By putting more on you, you may find it enables the listener hear your concerns less defensively.

Also, take responsibility for any contribution you've made to the problem that's legit. Ask for their views.

"No one can make you feel inferior without your consent."

Eleanor Roosevelt
1884 – 1962
political figure, activist, first lady

good listener traits

We don't always need a professional counselor but we do all need a good listener. You know you have one when you see these basic traits below. As with most things, if you want to find one, be one yourself.

listen to learn:

- *tune in* ... be free from distractions, don't interrupt, eye contact

- *be curious* ... ask clarifying questions, or restate what they've heard to verify, use attentive body language

- *withhold judgment* ... be open minded, don't prejudge or quickly jump into fix it strategies

emotions have layers

Assume that identifying and expressing emotions is not the end of the process ... you may just be on the outside layer. Emotions run deep and can hide well. Exposing one layer may be opening up the opportunity to discuss more. But consider that a good thing because you can't control something that you're not aware of.

"Our depth of connection is consistent with our depth of communication."

Raeb

emotions and connections

Consider the possibility that emotional connectedness is a function of emotional openness.

My friend James (already mentioned in this book) is a much sought-after speaker. He's well known for his ability to connect with his audience. He puts them at ease and touches hearts ... what every speaker would hope for.

I asked him how he does that, what makes him different in this area?

He said instantly, "Vulnerability is the key." His simple response stuck with me and as he explained it further, it changed my thinking. I'll paraphrase his comments the best I can.

"Most speakers try to impress. They try to show off trophies in humble brags, try to make themselves look worthy of being listened to. But when we hear others putting themselves on a pedestal, we instinctively want to knock them off or find the blemish in their shiny exterior. It's a natural reaction and it's a disconnect.

But when a speaker shows weakness, or fear, or struggle, or failure ... the listener is drawn in because they can relate. They naturally start pulling for that speaker. They want him to win."

being liked vs being loved

Let's apply that same concept to friendships.

We all know lots of people. Why is it that some we feel very close to and others not so much? There are some whose personal struggle feels much like our own ... whose loss would deeply affect us. And yet for others it's not the same.

We're not going to find one equation that explains it all, but we know that the difference isn't time or proximity. We can be around others for years without feeling close. And it's not a function of respect. We can appreciate a person's many good qualities, but not feel emotionally connected.

I'm suggesting that the connection between to people is in proportion to the emotional vulnerability we've shared.

If we share from the surface, we'll connect on the surface. If we share more deeply ... we'll connect on that deeper level.

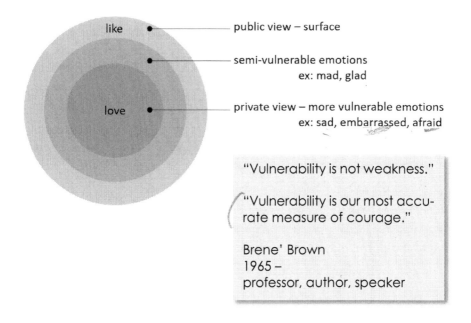

like ● — public view – surface

● — semi-vulnerable emotions
ex: mad, glad

love ● — private view – more vulnerable emotions
ex: sad, embarrassed, afraid

"Vulnerability is not weakness."

"Vulnerability is our most accurate measure of courage."

Brene' Brown
1965 –
professor, author, speaker

"We might impress people with our strengths, but we connect with people through our weaknesses."

Craig Groeshel
1967 –
pastor, author

emotions and vulnerability

Of the 5 Continuums of Emotion ... mad and glad tend to require the least vulnerability. We can often share those with minimal risk.

> "Loneliness does not come from having no people around you, but from being unable to communicate the things that are important to you."
>
> Carl Jung
> 1875 – 1961
> Swiss psychiatrist

The other 3 emotions tend to re-quire more vulnerability. Sharing what makes us sad, embarrassed, or afraid ... has more at stake. Those emotions can make us look weak, or less than in control, or less put together.

But the paradox is that we are naturally more attractive ... the less at-tractive we are. That can be taken out of context, but the truth in the statement comes from the fact that none of us are flawless and we naturally connect with others whom we can relate to.

I had one paper left to graduate from college, but this one was a year-long independent study worth 2 semesters grades. 120 pages had to be typed, and I couldn't type. Mary Anderson, a good friend who was engaged to my friend James, volunteered to help (not the same James). With herculean effort and legendary unselfishness, she got me across the finish line and is esteemed by my family to this day.

I'm embarrassed to remember what this task asked of her. As we struggled through, we had some significant peaks and valleys. What stands out in reflection is how we shared openly during those ups and downs. The last push was an all-nighter. We talked and prayed and cried and persevered, and finally made it. She was amazing.

Six months later, I was in my apartment in a new town with a small group from church. It was the week that Mary and James were to be married. I got a call which I took in my back bedroom. My friend Henry said sit down, there's been a terrible tragedy. Mary's family was flying in for the wedding on a Cessna and it had gone down. Her mom and dad were killed, her brother was on life support. Unimaginable.

I can never forget how that news bent me over in pain ... as if I was feeling some small bit of her agony and heartbreak. I cried so deeply for her. I couldn't fathom her grief, nor get myself back into the room with my friends. They eventually came looking for me. I was embarrassed at my inability to pull it together. Of all people, why her?

The depth of my reaction was peculiar to me then, and I'm finding the same now, all these years later. Each time I've gone over this part of the manuscript ... the tears have flowed so easily. I've wondered why such emotion. I don't have the final answer on that, but I believe it has to do with how Mary empathized with my emotions, and how she shared so vulnerably of her own. We interacted on a core level of emotion and a deeper trust and connection occurred as a result.

I'm honored to note her in this book ... which I am typing myself. :]

emotions at work

Not surprisingly, a big factor in how long people stick in a job is dependent on whether or not they have real friends on the team. We need connections at work also. More business decisions than we care to admit are influenced by our connections ... and what builds friendships outside of work does the same inside.

Work settings differ in their level of safety and we have to gauge what fits within our environment. Gushing vulnerabilities without restraint is not the point. But, changing any environment from closed to open does start somewhere. Change needs an initiator, a risk taker.

make it safe to speak on an emotional level

A work culture of openness and authenticity has a long list of benefits: co-workers' connections increase, support improves, better ideas emerge, problems are identified and solved quicker, co-worker engagement and longevity improves ... to name a few.

Authenticity isn't created by a poster on the wall. A few suggestions:

set the example ... Share at the level you would like to see coworkers sharing. Someone has to jump in the water first. Be that person.

identify unsafe behaviors ... Ask enough questions to know what makes your team or group a safe or unsafe place to speak up in.

engage opinion leaders ... Know who the opinion leaders are and hear their recommendations. Be open, create connections with them.

give options ... We don't all speak up the same. Some will in a large group, others never would. Create options for people to voice their opinions: small group (3 or 4), one on one conversations, email, etc.

leadership loyalty vs compliance

When a leader is open and authentic, they also build connections ... and those connections build loyalty.

Being a well-polished leader may garner admiration and respect, which is good ... and people will do what you ask. But loyalty comes through something deeper. People intrinsically know that you have to be strong to share weakness. It's an endearing quality.

> "Leadership consists of nothing but taking responsibility for things that go wrong and giving your subordinates credit for everything that goes well."
>
> Dwight Eisenhower
> 1890 – 1969
> five-star general, Supreme Commander Allied Forces, US President 1953-1961

a dialogue exercise

The goal of this activity is to build stronger connections through seeing more what stirs each other within. It could be used for teams or personal relationship building.

A) Each person writes their personal responses to the 5 emotion category questions: What might I be mad, sad, glad, embarrassed, or afraid about?

- *Mad*: What wrong(s) anger or nag at me?
- *Sad*: What loss could I be feeling?
- *Glad*: What am I very appreciative of?
- *Embarrassed*: Where do I feel I am below my expectations?
- *Afraid*: What threatens me or people I care about?

B) Then in groups of 2 or 3, participants share their responses with others. You can then combine groups, or come back into a large group to hear from others. Ask what the process felt like, and for their insights along the way.

C) Listeners: remember these 3 good listener traits
- *tune in* – show interest in hearing
- *be curious* – ask clarifying questions
- *withhold judgment* – not a time to oppose or correct

Let the conversation evolve.

"Vulnerability is the way back to each other."

Brene' Brown
1965 –
professor, author, speaker

3 controlling emotions

How we manage our emotions impacts every aspect of our lives. Careers and relationships are won or lost on this trait.

Anyone can be cordial and well-mannered in good times. It's how we respond under strong emotion that more accurately reveals what's beneath our public view.

"The measure of who we are is how we react to something that doesn't go our way."

Gregg Popovich
1949 –
NBA head coach, USA national team head coach

When a leader can't be trusted to control their emotions, that's a barrier. We may like them, respect them, and know they mean well ... but if they don't control their emotions, they're unpredictable and unsafe and we'll keep the necessary distance from them.

Conversely, when a leader consistently demonstrates emotional stability under trying times ... that they'll make decisions with reason and principle, over feeling or reaction ... then coworkers (and friends and family) see this person as a rock.

"We all have inner demons to fight. We call these demons 'fear' and 'hatred' and 'anger'."

"If you don't conquer them then a life of a hundred years is a tragedy. If you do then a life of a single day can be a triumph."

Ip Man
1893 – 1972
martial arts grandmaster, legend, mentor to Bruce lee

a leader's demeanor sets a tone

There's no escaping that a leaders' manner and disposition influences the culture of the team. So, managing emotions is an important topic in leading teams, people … and for leadership longevity.

Michael Jordan, 1982 NCAA National Championship game

This shot determined the 1982 NCAA national championship game. In the background, you see the benches of 2 very successful coaches (John Thompson and Dean Smith) but with different styles and personalities.

"Calm is contagious."

Tony Bennett
1969 –
UVA head basketball coach, national champion

The differences are not right vs wrong, just a reflection that a leader's demeanor certainly influences team culture and behavior.

emotions and decisions

We make every decision with some combination of reason and emotion. Both have their assets and liabilities, and good decision-makers find the right balance for the situation they're in.

It's good to know that emotions tend to be more powerful than reason, and can easily dominate decision making. They come from the core of our brain (amygdala) and were especially valuable for our hunter / gatherer days in life or death situations.

Fast forward a few years to the modern life we now live ... and instead of decisions in the wild, we're trying to get reach consensus with group of co-workers with different perspectives. In those moments, emotions can be just as strong but much less helpful.

overuses

So, paying attention to the need of the moment matters. Spock, for example, would be highly appreciated on a trip through space, but much less so on a spontaneous weekend jaunt to the beach.

We may be overly focused on logic when the need of the moment is more relational. Or, we can be swayed by a belief that our emotion equals truth, yet it only equals what we believe to be true. For example, I can be convinced that because I feel embarrassed, I must've done something embarrassing. That circular reasoning is not helpful.

It's a major step to become more aware of what is influencing our decision making between emotion or reason. The more aware we are, the less unhelpful influence either can have on us.

mind → emotion → will

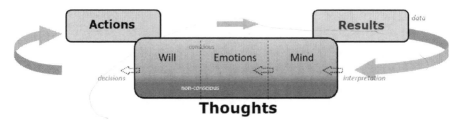

The Cause and Effect Spiral© in more detail regarding Thoughts

Note: No brains were harmed in the making of this picture. It's not a real brain. It is also out of proportion. Real brain people tell us that about 95% of brain activity fits in the non-conscious, not a third as is roughly represented here.

Mind ... we instantly analyze and interpret objective data to 'understand'. It answers questions like ... What is this? What does this mean? We develop our understanding and reasoning here.

Emotion ... is our (energy moving through the body) reaction to our interpretations or beliefs.

Will ... is our ability to choose, our free will. It is not the same as interpreting data (deciding what something means). Here we determine our best action, using reason &/or emotion.

a near death experience

I was with 3 friends on a backpacking trip in Virginia. It was dusk and we had just made our first camp in the wilderness of Grayson High-lands. Elwood and I decided to venture a bit outside our camp to see what was around us. It became difficult to see with the sun almost down, but then we spot something in the distance.

"The possibilities are numerous once we decide to act and not react."

George Bernard Shaw
1856 – 1950
Irish playwright, political activist

We then realized it was coming at us ... that it was not slowing down ... that it was big ... it was what we feared most ... a bear was charging!

My emotions revved up in to high gear. I ran a few steps but realized I couldn't get away. I stopped to prepare for contact. The fear and adrenaline were intense.

> "Fear is an emotion. Courage is a decision."
>
> Winston Churchill
> 1874 – 1965
> British Prime Minister, writer

As the animal approached (yes, all official bear attack strategies slipped my mind, including that I really only had to outrun Elwood.) and we prepared to be violently thrust into the next world ... we realized this ferocious bear was only a well-fattened pony hoping to be fed. We would live to see another day.

Now let's look at the 3 aspects of Thought in slow motion ... as they played out in my near-death pony licking experience:

> *Mind* ... I saw a charging object (data), I interpreted (reasoned) that to be a bear intent on doing harm

> *Emotion* ... in response to believing I'm in danger... adrenaline rushed in and my whole-body awareness was heightened

> *Will* ... I decided to run, then reasoned that was useless and decided to turn and fight (as if I could)

Presumably our present-day emotions are similar to those of our cave cousins even though our common challenges are not. The jolt of emotional electricity I received to survive my bear attack (turned overfed pony) ... was helpful in that moment. But, those same emotions in an office setting where the challenge is coming to agreement can be an obstacle. Making decisions require us to navigate two rivers of information flooding our brain for influence ... reason and emotion.

emotions are smart too

It's not that reason is smart ... and emotions are dumb. On the contrary, emotion can have a huge amount of intuitive information and validity, and 'reason' can be biased and ignorant. So, it's not just emotion that needs to be subverted at times to make a wise decision. Both reason and emotion can be a hindrance to making a wise decision.

> Be selective in your battles. Sometimes peace is better than being right.

It may not be 'reasonable' to turn the car around to go get the $2 teddy bear that flew out the window on a busy highway, or to spend $3K on a dog's operation. There are factors beyond the facts that can overrule reason. (Yes, we did turn around and get the teddy bear, and yes Mom did pay for the operation).

balance is not necessarily the goal

A 50-50 balance between reason and emotion in making decision is not the goal. Rather, it's to be appropriate to the need of the moment.

A particular situation may require more consideration and empathy ... and we'd be out of touch if we don't read that well. Other decisions may require a strong emphasis on reasoning and critical thinking, to the exclusion of emotional factors.

Let's look at both reason and emotion in decisions.

reason in decisions

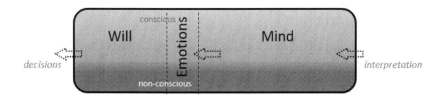

Reason is an *asset* when ...

> *accuracy and details matter* ... situations where precision, facts and evidence are needed to make logical decisions

> *bias is strong* ... when subjectivity is strongly swaying opinions and decisions based on favoritism or tribal thinking

"May your choices reflect your hopes, not your fears."

Nelson Mandela
1918 – 2013
anti-apartheid revolutionary leader, President South Africa

Reason is a *liability* when ...

> *quick action is needed* ... at times speed is more important than precision ... when done is better than perfect

> *spontaneity is valued* ... at times it's ok to not plan every step; instead explore and let things emerge that cannot be planned

> *innovation is needed* ... when failure is not fatal and new possibilities are needed ... reasoning can be a hindrance

Dad's advice

When Nancy and I were getting married, my mother got very deeply into helping us, and beautifully so.

She's been the hub of our family and a very good organizer. She has orchestrated multi-family beach trips yearly, large family reunions, high school reunions, was president of her local teacher's association, elder in her church, etc. She makes things happen. It's a gift.

Printing the invitations was my one job, and I did it as I thought was reasonable. I got 500 printed and paid for, and sent them off to Mom and Dad (4 hours away). A few days later they call, and I'm expecting them to really like the invitations. But it turned out … not so much. I had had my casual name printed, Bill (not William) and then left out my middle name. Mom wished I had used my full formal name. I responded kind of factually, 'Well, I go by Bill and never use my middle name. That's how my fiends know me. So, all good.' I left it at that.

A few days later Dad, my best man, called. He lovingly and skillfully shared some wisdom. Bottom line, he said … 'Some things are worth fighting for, but not everything. Learn to pick your battles. And sometimes you do something just because it's important to another.' He remined me that a lot of their friends and family would be getting these invitations and that this was a significant event for more than just Nancy and I. I was with him … sort of. But his next point got me.

He then reminded me where my middle name came from. It came from Mom's father. He was a girl dad and she was a daddy's girl, but sadly lost him at age 17. She named me for him and spoke glowingly of him all of my life. His name on the invitation going out to her family and friends meant a lot to her. I got it. We got all 500 reprinted. Dad was showing me that sometimes emotional / relational issues matter more than logical ones.

emotion in decisions

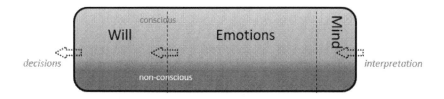

Emotion is an *asset when* …

> *we tune into our intuition* … a source of valuable information

> *we consider others* … their feelings, how the outcomes of a de-cision effect social or human factors around us

Emotion is a *liability* when …

> *it overrides our reasoning* … limiting our ability to connect ac-tions and consequences; strong emotions like anger, sadness, excitement, embarrassment, or fear can cloud thinking

> *we neglect responsibilities* … avoiding something unpleasant or doing something for instant gratification is harmful if we ne-glect other things that have important consequences

> *we put tribe over principle* … our innate need to belong can make us exceedingly subjective: we justify unfair tribal behav-ior that promotes uneven scales that favor us

examples of overly emotional decisions

- Sports fans going mad at calls that penalize their team ... yet in reverse would believe the same call is fine.

- In our polarized political scene, we justify our party doing something that we'd clearly oppose had it come from the other side.

- Not recognizing how often we've done the previous politically.

- A basketball coach has a son or daughter on the team to whom he offers preferential treatment.

- All-white juries across the south exonerating white defendants ... where a black defendant would never have walked free.

"The worst form of injustice is pretended justice."

Plato
~428BC – 348BC
Athenian philosopher, founded first higher learning institution in western culture

"Justice cannot be for one side alone, but must be for both."

Eleanor Roosevelt
1884 – 1962
political figure, activist, first lady

we're responsible for our emotions

Emotions can seem so uncontrollable, as if they have a mind of their own … like an out of control child on a plane that just won't behave. It's not uncommon to give emotions a pass, maybe because the hidden beliefs that trigger them are so well hidden.

Yet because emotions result from what we do control … our thoughts and perspectives … we're responsible for them. We don't get to blame emotions on something else. They are us.

My mother is now 85. Like most anyone in their 80's … she's had her challenges. Her memory is not the same, her independence is not the same, her daily company is not the same. She lost my dad years ago, and we just recently lost my older brother. Of her 2 sisters, both younger, one recently passed away and the other just had a serious stroke. Her life was significantly disrupted when we moved her from her home of 50 years in Chapel Hill to a senior living facility near Nancy and I. She's fighting her second bout with cancer.

 me

"Gettin' old aint for sissies."

my Uncle Bill

Yet, every ... single ... day .... she comments on how beautiful the sky is. Every day she finds the moon, or the clouds, or the birds, or the flowers, or the big old trees and the older homes. She still has wonder in her heart that shows on her face.

When anyone does something for her, she is so grateful and appreciative and her words say so. She's always wanting good for others. I see the choices she makes on what to look for in life, and the impact that has on her daily life, on her daily emotions.

We'd like to deny that we're responsible for our emotions. But we see that disproven in those around us who face major trials with grace and poise. They show us the fallacy of whining.

Those who choose the ugly opposite by being rude and obtuse, despite having more than their fair share of blessings ... demonstrate again that we find what we look for.

We get to choose, not just our actions, but our thoughts as well ... and feelings follow thoughts.

> "If our emotional abilities aren't in hand, if you don't have self-awareness, if you are not able to manage your distressing emotions, if you can't have empathy and have effective relationships, then no matter how smart you are, you are not going to go very far. "
>
> Daniel Goleman
> 1946 –
> author Emotional Intelligence

8 Beliefs

tell yourself a better truth

As we've said, nothing is more core to who we are ... than how we think. Thoughts bookend our actions ... first they direct them and then afterwards they interpret their results. Thoughts guide our rise or fall.

An important chunk of our thinking has to do with our continuous self-talk ... some we're conscious of, but most we are not. For example, we've come to believe that trees will stand as we walk past them, and that chairs will hold up as we sit in them ... and those beliefs guide our behavior without us paying any more attention to them.

Established beliefs are essential. They keep us from living the movie 'Fifty First Dates', relearning the same things over and over. They help us build and move forward. But because they are given diplomatic immunity to roam unchecked and unchallenged inside our thinking ... they can also be dangerous. When we establish beliefs that are negative or limiting, they do harm as our actions correlate with those downward thoughts.

> You will never speak to anyone more than you speak to yourself in your head. So be kind to yourself.
>
> unknown

87

For example, if we come to a belief that … I'm not worthy of being treated with respect … or, I will always be a low-level worker … or, I'm not capable of having a flourishing business … then they'll spawn actions consistent with those limiting thoughts.

self fulling prophecy

Let's mention shame. Brene' Brown says that guilt is believing my action was bad, but shame is believing that I am bad … a big difference. Shame is highly correlated with destructive behaviors like addiction, depression, violence, bullying, eating disorders, etc … but guilt is inversely associated with these same behaviors. So, the more I think a behavior is bad, the less I'll do it. But the more I think I'm bad, the more I'll do bad behaviors. What we believe about ourselves matters.

Fortunately, shame is not a trait, but a feeling that results from established negative beliefs, and beliefs can be changed.

overly certain

Established beliefs are things we are certain of. When we're certain, we tend to stop asking questions … we think we've got it. But being easily certain also makes us easily gullible. An easily certain mindset is fertile soil for bigotry or other ignorations. To grow and change, it's important to question our thinking, to continually add better truths. We have to keep making space in the cup to pour in more tea.

"Don't ask the person with all the answers, ask the person with all the questions. "

Albert Einstein
1879 – 1955
German physicist

tribal beliefs

We are all apart of some tribe with its pattern of thinking and acting. That particular culture … on our small dot of the world, in our thin slice of world history … heavily influences our worldview and is the lens through which we make sense of the world.

Developing a shared mindset is not all bad. We can learn a lot of good from each other, and build connection. But we can also allow a lot of ignorant views to go unchallenged. Our thinking needs to be continually rethunked ... or group think becomes group stink.

For example: The tribe of Hitler saw Jews as unworthy of life on their earth ... In 1955, a white community tribe in Mississippi was complicit in exonerating 2 white men who had abducted, tortured and murdered a 14 year-old black teenager, Emmett Till, for whistling at a white lady ... The Taliban tribe concluded that women should not work, be educated, or be seen unveiled ... The mainstream America tribe until recently saw women as only homemakers and not fit for stressful decision-making jobs, or strenuous athletics ... and on and on. So, while tribal thinking is common and essential, unchecked it's limiting and dangerous.

unlearning

Imbedded truths are difficult to uproot, but our brains can adapt. As we repeat new thinking and actions, our brain builds fresh neuron pathways and eliminates old ones. If we get hooked on Diet Coke, but then change our habits to drinking water ... brain changes occur and we can soon crave water. We have 'unlearned' our craving for soda and replaced it with something healthier.

In our context, we're unlearning beliefs that hinder us ... which involves identifying, refuting and replacing them, and that has to do with our self-talk.

> "Those who cannot change their mind cannot change anything. "
>
> George Bernard Shaw
> 1856 – 1950
> Irish playwright, political activist

Self-talk has a profound impact. I want to re-emphasis the concept to make sure it's on our radar.

Self-talk is our ongoing monologue of thought, consciously and non-consciously, that triggers emotions and directs behavior. While we can talk out loud maybe at 150-200 words a minute, some suggest that we can self-talk about 1300 words a minute. We tell ourselves a lot.

Plenty of research supports that successful people choose more positive thoughts than those who are not as successful. Negative thoughts are present within everyone, but the difference is in how well we override the negative.

refute and replace

To improve our self-talk … it's a great help to be in tune with negative emotions because they lead us directly to the negative thought(s) triggering them. Once in the light, we can refute and replace the negative thoughts with a better, more constructive truth. We'll get into that more in the next chapter with Raeb Mapping.

"The greatest weapon against stress is our ability to choose one thought over another. "

William James
1842 – 1910
father of American psychology

we find what we look for

The point is that we carry with us each day ... an ability to choose our focus. Some days are more difficult than others, but we always remain capable of, and responsible for controlling our thinking.

In training sessions, to make this point ... sometimes I'll ask the group to take 30 seconds to go find anything yellow. It's always impressive how much they're able to find when they focus. If we're outside, it's usually leaves with color in them. If inside, it's pointing out things on the wall or to someone's clothes.

We then discuss the value of focus and apply that to some concept for the day. Sometimes it's to look for the good in others, or variations in leadership styles, or how the group is making decisions, etc. But the point is, we find what we look for.

So self-talk both comes from and determines our mental focus. Taking control of our lives means taking control of our self-talk. Let's look at a way to improve that.

"We are always paid for our suspicions by finding what we suspect."

Henry David Thoreau
1817 – 1862
American naturalist, essayist

"Men are disturbed, not by things, but by the view they take of them."

Epictetus
55 – 135 AD
Greek philosopher

"People will take you as seriously as you take yourself."

Jon Goodman
friend, wealth advisor

from another's point of view

Each year I get to be a part of a program working with incoming MBA students at Duke Fuqua School of Business, from the younger day time group to the more experienced global executives.

This year, as part of connecting on a deeper level, I asked two of my executive level groups, to finish this sentence: (One thing I know for sure is ....)? They would then elaborate.

As they began to answer I was intrigued by their comments and asked permission to take notes and possibly share later. This is how all 24 finished the sentence.

- I can do anything I want to.
- I'm going to have to continue to learn the rest of my life.
- I can expect change, so embrace it.
- Tomorrow is a new day.
- There's always room for improvement and lots of ways to do things.
- I have to surround myself with people more intelligent than I am.
- Anything is possible.
- This too shall pass.
- I control my life.
- Gratitude determines my outlook on life.
- We'll have fun.
- Things aren't as important as they seem.

- Nothing. I try not to know anything for sure and to question my thought process.
- I need to always be a good dad.
- There is such power in developing meaningful relationships.
- We all own our own success.
- That I don't know anything (from a medical doctor)
- Whatever it is, I will do it. Persistence is what matters.
- The only constant is change, so we have to adapt.
- That I have a lot to learn.
- You're the captain of your own ship. If you're not taking control of your life someone else will.
- Weak things break.
- I'm not alone, tap into relationships.
- We're all going to die.

peek

Well, maybe not all responses were book worthy. But I bet you too can benefit from a peak into some thoughts from successful folks. Success is not by accident. What we allow to dominate our thoughts makes a significant difference.

Maybe when you face a tough day or challenge, come to this list and see if any of these mindsets would be helpful to adopt.

"Could a greater miracle take place than for us to look through each other's eyes for an instant."

Henry David Thoreau
1817 – 1862
American naturalist, essayist

93

9 Raeb Mapping

objective reflection

Raeb had a simple and effective way to help others to get unstuck, or to make needed improvements.

His technique was a 5-minute refection to map cause and effect in the 4 areas (chapters we just reviewed) ... Results, Actions, Emotions, and Beliefs ... and then make small doable changes in one or more of these. This is not to turn a coach into a therapist (one who delves deeply into causes and reasons), but rather to provide a meaningful view of what's creating current realities.

Two things set the stage for effective mapping. First, get specific on an issue or area in your life to map. And second ... put yourself in a spectator role, observing your life from afar. Objectivity is key.

From there you reflect on NOW, what's creating what you see ... and then NEW ... what changes would create what you want to see.

Let's look at the 4 areas of Raeb Mapping.

Raeb Mapping – 5 minutes / 8 questions

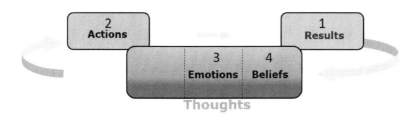

		a) now	b) new	
Part 1	**1** **Results**	my results are ...	my expectations are ...	external
	2 **Actions**	my actions are ...	I could do ...	
Part 2	**3** **Emotions**	I feel ...	I expect to feel ...	internal
	4 **Beliefs**	I'm telling myself ...	a better truth is ...	

Whatever we are not changing, we are choosing. Raeb

clarifications

Set up:
- identify the specific area you are analyzing
- become an objective observer of your own life

2 columns:
   a = now (what you are currently experiencing)
   b = new (what you want to experience)

Write answers, don't just think them through. The process of writing forces choice and is another level of experience with those thoughts.

Work either down the columns or across rows. Do what feels most comfortable for you. Be aware that Part 1: Results and Actions… are external, observable by others. Part 2: Emotions and Beliefs … are internal, coming from within.

1. *Results*
   a. My current results are:
   b. My expected results are:
2. *Actions*
   a. My actions generating these results are:
   b. My actions needed for better results are:
3. *Emotions*
   a. I'm feeling:
   b. I want to feel:
4. *Beliefs*
   a. I'm telling myself: (beliefs triggering the emotion)
   b. A better truth would be: (refute and replace old beliefs)

more a process than an event

Raeb Mapping is not meant to be a one-off event, but an ongoing series of short reflections. Beliefs and emotions in particular are often well camouflaged and thus uncovered in layers.

So, have a place to capture these insights. Start simply with a page on a notepad where you create the 2 columns (now and new) and 4 rows (results, actions, emotions, beliefs), adding pages as needed.

Then, capture your insights that come from your 5 min reflections, as well as the ones that hit you as you go about your day. Look for patterns and see where they lead you.

> "You can't hit what you can't see."
>
> Walter Johnson
> 1887 – 1946
> Hall of Fame MLB pitcher

Don't expect it to be easy at first, it is a process. It's learning to see something you've not been paying too much attention to. But the more you look, the better you'll get at spotting negative thoughts and feelings and actions ... and the better you can refute and replace them.

why not give it a shot right now?

You only need pen and paper and a few minutes.

Action!

Create 8 blocks on a page. Identify a specific area where you want better results. And then see what comes to mind.

Don't labor over your answers, just jot initial thoughts. They're not final answers. You can add or subtract later as you see consistency developing.

why Raeb Mapping works

The belief that we are unable to control our results is a root cause of much frustration, discouragement, and even depression. When we want something but come to believe that we can't get it ... we feel helpless.

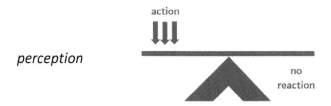

But as we see our cause and effect, it's freeing. Even seeing we're the cause of our own negative results is empowering. Identifying a cause is also revealing a fix, and that puts us back in the game.

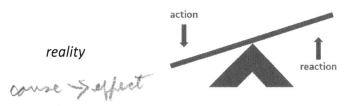

The clearer we see cause and effect, the better we can respond. When I grasp that my unmet expectation is the result of my attitudes and actions, despite the weight of responsibility, I'll at least see that I'm in control. To shield ourselves or another from cause and effect is unnatural and unhelpful. Raeb Mapping uncovers that connection.

When you remove the struggle, you remove the learning.

additional considerations

identify unhelpful thought patterns, such as:
- all or none ... overly conclusive, black/white thinking ... instead, see gray areas or alternative meanings
- feelings equal truth ... emotion driven thinking ... instead, acknowledge new content, facts, or evidence
- finding the bad ... hyper focus on imperfections ... instead, see small wins and learn from mistakes

tell off a friend
- write a negative thought(s) you've told yourself about yourself
- now say this in an imaginary conversation to a good friend, using the same tones and attitudes you use toward yourself
- reflect: Would I actually speak that way to someone I care about? What messages am I sending? How would I prefer to come across? How can I speak to myself better?

> "Angels whisper to a man when he goes for a walk."
>
> unknown

to better reflect
- go for a walk, get away from your office or computer
- take a drive going nowhere, country roads maybe
- talk things over with a friend ... hearing yourself expressing thoughts and feeling out loud can give new perspective
- interview someone with a very different perspective than your own ... 'ask to learn'
- take new small action steps and see what changes
- get out of town for a brief escape

Now, let's shift into applying these same principles into coaching strategies using the Adaptive Coaching Model.

Part

3

Adaptive Coaching

10 – Coaching Style
11 – Coaching Focus
12 – Adaptive Coaching Model©

Part 3 builds the Adaptive Coaching model with 2 main components ... Coaching Styles (Directive, Facilitative, and Delegative) ... and Coaching Focus (Competence, Confidence, and Motivation).

The AC model is organized common sense, capturing what we do when we coach well. Its value is in providing you a guide to make accurate decisions on how to best coach those you lead, as their needs change.

10 Coaching Style

A participant in a recent leadership program commenting on how they are being coached at work said, "When people just tell you what to do, it kills your confidence in yourself and then you do stupid things."

What this person was identifying was the harm done by out of sync coaching styles ... in this case micro-managing. Coaching mismatches are not only not a help, they're a hindrance. They hold people back.

Leaning heavily on a particular go-to style of coaching style is like driving a car that won't shift gears. It's perfect in some situations but a limitations in others.

Long term leadership effectiveness is connected to the ability to adjust to changing needs. Adaptive Coaching is about knowing when and how to make these shifts.

3 Performance Levels

Before we get into 3 specific coaching styles … let's identify how to categorize the co-worker performance. We'll rank <u>current</u> performance (<u>of a specific task</u>) to be at one of 3 levels:

Level 3 = Successful

success, is going well and either is now or will soon reach a
high level if continued

Level 2 = Moderately Successful

some success, yet inconsistent,
not sustained … some up and
some down

Level 1 = Unsuccessful

not successful, not working,
continuing in this direction
would be unacceptable.

Next, we'll look at which coaching style fits naturally with each of these 3 Performance Level.

Performance Levels are on the left (1,2, and 3) each with a matching coaching style (Direct, Facilitate, and Delegate). A leader's involvement lessens as the coworker's effectiveness increases.

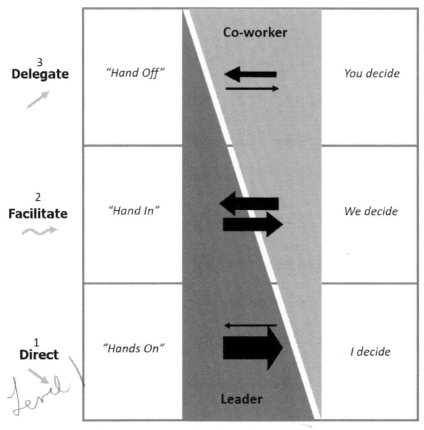

©Bill Winfrey 2018 – Adaptive Coaching Style Continuum

Let's talk about each level in a bit more detail.

Level 1 → Direct

Whether your co-worker sees it or not, their performance spiral is heading downward. This is not working. The need of the moment is for you to be 'Hands On', to be directive on how things need to be done. A change is needed, and pretty soon if not immediately.

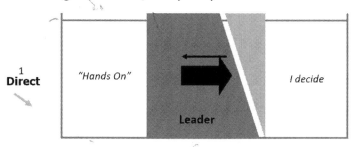

When you Direct ... you'll do more telling than asking ... give clear progressive, step by step instructions (micro-managing actually is a fit here) ... decisions are basically up to you (get input as appropriate).

Beware of ... becoming disrespectful, belittling, being impatient, etc. Leaders often take the directing style as a license to talk down, maybe believing this style requires it. It does not.

Being human is worthy of respect, if only for that reason alone. Your ability to show respect reflects on you, not them. In reverse, don't confuse their compliance to your authority as respect. Earn respect and loyalty by how you treat people, more so than from a title.

It is entirely possible to be demanding without being demeaning, and that's 80% tone. Much of a leader's reputation is defined by their ability to balance these complexities.

> "The respect you show is not a reflection on their character, but your own."
>
> Raeb

.

Here, the performance spiral is not distinctly heading up or down ... or if so, it's waffling a bit. The appropriate style then is Facilitating, where you have a 'Hand in', but are not so large and in charge as before. You've let go of one hand, but still holding on with the other.

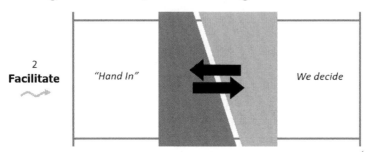

2
Facilitate   *"Hand In"*   *We decide*

When you Facilitate ... you'll do less instructing and more dialogue, less telling and more asking. Your co-worker has demonstrated some success, so ask questions and let them speak. Make decisions that have more agreement. You still have the final say, but loosen the reins.

Beware of ... your own tendencies. If you're not naturally a facilitative personality, this approach will feel awkward. As your co-worker is stretching, so are you. If you tend to ...

- *direct* ... be aware of your 'need' to control ... and don't 'steal the learning'. They learn through their own experience, not your words. So back off and let them make some mistakes. Don't just have two gears, on or off. Find the in-between gear, and make friends with its awkward-ness.

  > "Don't steal the learning."
  >
  > Jane Vella
  > 1931 –
  > author, founder Global Learning Partners

- *delegate* ... don't back off too soon. Stay engaged with your co-worker by in-itiating conversations and watching them think things through via your dialogue.

Level 3 → Delegate

Here the spiral is heading upward nicely. The work is being done well and success is showing. Delegating is now appropriate.

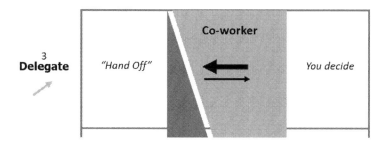

When you Delegate ... you're giving your co-worker the responsibility to make decisions and to bring results. You don't disappear, because the results still have your name on them.

Instead, you clarify the goal line (expectations), any out of bounds lines (limits) ... but let them call the plays. You become like a team owner who observes from up in the booth ... while letting them play the game. An ability (willingness) to 'let go' is often the difference between growth or stagnation.

Beware of ...
- micro-managing ... It's easy to be overly involved when you have a high performer, which you know stunts growth and motivation. So back off and let this person learn through experience as you have.
- being absent ... Instead, remain connected, track progress.

"The best leaders create more leaders, not just followers."

Raeb

"The greatest sign of success for a teacher is to be able to say 'The children are now working as if I do not exist.' "

Maria Montessori
1879 – 1952
educator

What helps and what hinders in each of the coaching styles.

	Helps	Hinders
Delegate	More follower led decisions Ask and listen often Encouraging autonomy ... allowing their differences & preferences Monitoring progress Remaining accessible Continuing to challenge them with next level goals	Overmanaging, micro-managing Following your need to provide answers, vs allowing their need to discover Not listening well Not providing the big picture Minimal connection to consequences Disengaging, abandoning
Facilitate	2-way dialogue Encourage questions and input Discuss reasons and details Give a growing number of steps, but not a hand off Support risk taking, mistakes ok Increase follower made decisions	Dominating conversations Railroading your agenda Long lectures, over teaching Not taking time to answer questions Keeping a tight rein, in control Leaving alone, disengaging Punishing failure when effort was good
Direct	Mostly one way, instruction-led communication Provide specifics: who, what, where, when, how Incremental instructions, don't overwhelm Closely supervise Find the good Constructive Feedback – correct without demeaning Keep negative emotions in check (anger, frustration, impatience, etc.)	Lots of talk ... little action or opportunity to experience Being short, unclear on details Making steps too big Taking small steps of progress for granted, not acknowledging progress Demean or disrespect in your correcting Back off too soon, assuming they've got it

11 Coaching Focus

Now that we have a basic framework to guide coaching style, the next question is ... WHERE do we focus our coaching efforts?

High performance is a result of multiple factors. In getting to high performance ... it's important to know which is needed most now, because they vary.

Let's use athletics. When you're coaching athletes, the current need might be 'how-to' instruction from you ... they are eager but simply don't know what to do. At another time, the issue may be belief in their ability. At another time, the issue may be about motivation ... they know and are confident but are not willing to put the effort in.

Those interventions are not the same ... and a mismatch can be an obstruction. A basketball coach getting overly stern (yelling) at a player who's eager but needs instruction ... is counter-productive.

There is some rhyme and reason on what to focus on when. That's what this chapter is about.

To clarify 3 areas of focus … let's go back to the Cause & Effect Spiral©. A positive nudge of any of these 3 components can tilt a performance spiral upwards.

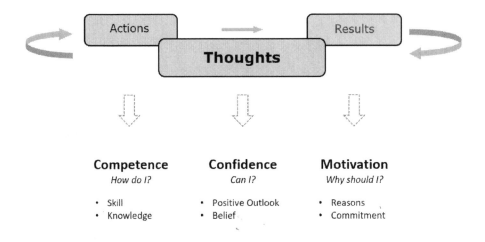

Competence	Confidence	Motivation
How do I?	*Can I?*	*Why should I?*
• Skill	• Positive Outlook	• Reasons
• Knowledge	• Belief	• Commitment

The 3 components of the spiral manifest as:

- Actions → Competence (issues of skill or knowledge)

- Thoughts → Confidence (issues of faulty thinking)

- Results → Motivation (issues of results mattering)

A co-worker shifting a downward spiral into an upward one ... will be directly connected to changing one of these 3 factors.

Competence	Confidence	Motivation
How do I?	*Can I?*	*Why should I?*
• Skill	• Positive Outlook	• Reasons
• Knowledge	• Belief	• Commitment

A little further look into each performance factor.

1. **Competence** ... is the ability to perform the task. That could be balancing a budget or giving a speech or anything needed. Sometimes the missing piece has to do with a skill, and sometimes it could be having sufficient information.

2. **Confidence** ... is having a secure belief in my own ability to get the job done. I may have good skills, yet lack confidence in my ability ... usually because of inexperience. It is common for confidence to lag behind skill.

3. **Motivation** ... means that the results matter to me, a lot. That I have my own personal reasons for performing at a high level, and I am committed to doing so.

Some reminders of subtleties that make a difference in each.

	Competence	Confidence	Motivation
Helps			
	Clarify expectations Explain in detail (relative to what they can take in) Teach at their pace Check for retention Provide all resources needed Model behaviors / skills Incremental skill development Constructive feedback	Express your belief Focus on effort Make mistakes learnings Commend in private & public Ask their opinions Correct objectively Entrust / Challenge	Discuss big picture … (purpose, vision, impacts) Involve them as an essential contributor Ensure challenge or 'stretch' is appropriate – (not too much or too little) Connect to consequences (good or bad)
Hinders			
	Be impatient (short, annoyed with their pace) Vague instructions Expect that telling is teaching (they need to do and get constructive feedback) Assume that what's easy for you is easy for them	Demean for mistakes Challenge / Stretch too far Punish for mistakes (when effort is good) Correct in anger Create 'dog houses' Not find the good Shoot down ideas or comments or innovation	Over manage Overload (with more due to their success) Detach them from the rewards or consequences of their results Allow 'distractions' that effect performance Take them for granted, fail to recognize Disengage

3 independent factors ... These factors can be present in any combination. A co-worker having one of these does not assure they do or do not have any of the others. Below are some variations.

	Competence	Confidence	Motivation
	How do I?	*Can I?*	*Why should I?*
a)	✓	X	X
b)	X	✓	X
c)	X	X	✓

each factor needs a different approach ... While each factor benefits from development in the others, they each need their own unique focus and attention. The specifics of what build competence or confidence or motivation are not exactly the same. Treat them as stand alone issues despite the fact that they do overlap.

missing any will drop performance ... Even if a co-worker has excellent competence, if either of the others are lacking, then performance and their reliability is lacking something important. A deficiency in any is a performance block. They may eventually overcome weak areas on their own without your help, but your role as coach is to facilitate that process ... making it more likely and less lengthy.

it takes all 3 to be a high performer... When a co-worker has competence, confidence, and motivation it's time to get out of the way. If one is lacking it's worth noting and shifting your coaching strategy.

12 The Adaptive Coaching Model©

The difference between a model and theory is that a model guides decision making, a theory does not. A theory is a general statement about a phenomenon ... while a model is a purposeful representation of reality. We can talk all night about the Big Bang Theory but it is not likely to guide many decisions the next day.

The AC model is to help guide your decisions on how to adjust your coaching based on the co-worker's needs.

A few years ago, I inquired at the Center for Creative Leadership cafeteria who made the tuna salad. I was told it was Ernie, a lady everyone loves. I asked her how she made it, hoping to repeat it at home. Ernie said with a big smile ... "I put the love it in!" That's all she gave me, but that was a lot. Her phrase is now common around our house.

I see Ernie's recipe relating here. A good model can point us in the right direction, but it's only a framework, we have to add the love ... the relationship, the intuition, the personality. Maybe it's us that make the difference, not some model.

builds from the Cause & Effect Spiral©

You'll see that the AC model comes from and builds upon the simplicity of the C&E Spiral.

114

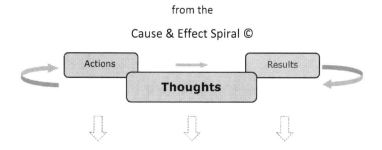

from the

Cause & Effect Spiral ©

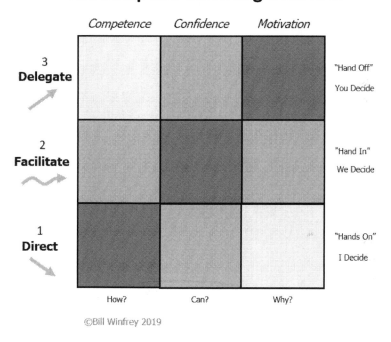

The Adaptive Coaching Model ©

©Bill Winfrey 2019

The darker the shade of gray, the greater the focus. Let's look more closely at the primary focus for each performance level.

Style → Directive

In this particular task, Fred is not getting the job done. His work is turned in late and has below par quality. This is an important task within his role. It's important for the team and for Fred's longevity, that he get this right. You step in to create change and here that means your style will be Directive ... 'Hands On'.

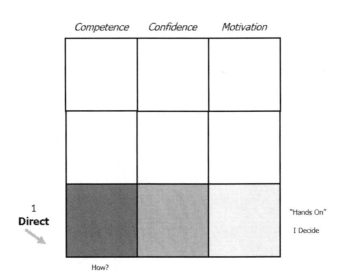

While you'll need to first ask and listen to get an accurate understanding of the situation and it's causes ... it's appropriate for you to soon be doing more telling than asking, even dictating how things get done. But bottom line, this task needs to be done differently.

How you do that matters. It's possible to be demanding without being demeaning. Consider that tone is 80% of your communication and that it will also determine whether you're gaining or losing loyalty.

Focus → Competence

At the same time, at Level 1, you skip the part where you're playing wonderful counselor, looking for the perfect words to encourage or inspire. Instead, trust that their newfound positive actions (and the good results that follow), will be an even better 'counselor'.

So, your most urgent focus now is to get them doing things well, doing the right actions … so they experience positive results.

Break the task into appropriate steps. Stay closely involved to see that each step is done well. Be available to demonstrate or explain the actions needed and to provide objective feedback and guidance.

Your primary focus here is not on Confidence and Motivation, but you still touch on them. Remind them that you believe in them and why the results are important … but don't camp out there. Keep your focus on how you can get them to *experience* positive action.

What if a co-worker has regressed to level 1?

Regression is not the same as progression. If after being at Level 2 or 3 … there is a drop back to Level 1, then something's up. It's not that they can't, they've already demonstrated they can. So have a conversation to uncover what's going on. You'll likely be identifying confidence or motivation issues.

Allow failure

We all have to fail to learn. It's our teacher. If nothing else, it teaches us we need input. Be ok backing off and letting failure happen. Remain close enough to ensure that *failure is not fatal.* Be there to teach. Make it a learning experience, not an 'I told you so' put down.

Style → Facilitate

At Level 2, your co-worker has displayed some solid performance, so they are not at Level 1. But something is keeping performance from being Level 3. Maybe it's inconsistency, maybe it's a lack of confidence, or a missing motivation piece.

For whatever reason, they are not ready to for a handoff, but neither do they need you to be overly directive. So you're style is facilitative.

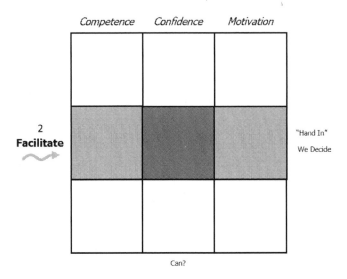

So on a separate task Fred is at Level 2. Generate conversation to uncover answers and then get agreement by both of you sharing ideas and solutions. Allow the decision to be mutual ... even at times going with his idea though you're pretty certain yours is better. You're grooming Fred to take responsibility without you. So be willing to let him learn through experience ...

just as you have.

> When you remove the struggle, you remove the learning.

Focus → Confidence

When a co-worker is yet to be highly successful in a task, a common question is 'Can I?'. An insightful coach can often see potential well before they do. They've yet to have the opportunity to build the confidence that comes only through personal experience.

So here, focus initially and primarily on helping them build Confidence. Give them reason to believe they can do it. Your words and insights from you experience mean a lot. Don't wait for them to tell you they need a confidence boost. Inspire them to take the next actions that they may be hesitant on.

why not motivation before confidence?

Hitting on motivation first would not be wrong ... especially if you sense motivation to be the main issue. The AC model is not suggesting that you forget the other 2 factors not currently highlighted.

The model is, however, suggesting you focus on confidence ahead of motivation in a common skill progression scenario ... for 2 reasons. One, assume people have some basic motivation to do their job well ... it's what they're paid to do. And two, because building some experience-based confidence often helps develop motivation. If after building some competence and confidence on a work-related task, and they are not motivated, then shift to motivation issues.

regression is different

When a Level 3 performer is now at Level 2, then motivation is certainly a place to look. Something has changed, and while it could be and event or failure that has shaken confidence ... it could also be burnout that is eating away at motivation. Check both.

Style → Delegate

At Level 3, your co-worker has shown they've got it. They have demonstrated competence, confidence, and motivation.

	Competence	Confidence	Motivation	
3 **Delegate**				"Hand Off" You Decide
2				

Why?

So, be clear about big picture expectations and deadlines ... and boundaries they have to work within. But then let them figure it out from there.

Provide any necessary resources and be within reach if they need your opinion. But don't assume that they need you to swoop in and save the day. Instead, facilitate a conversation and let them decide. Help them realize how capable they are of figuring things out ... versus you showing them how capable you are.

Focus → Motivation

You have a high performer who can handle the task. The fact that they are not as experienced as you, or may not do it exactly as you would is no reason to keep hold of the reins. That's your issue, not theirs. Back off and allow them the same opportunity you've had to learn from your own experiences and mistakes.

Challenge itself is motivating, so create it for them. Just pay attention that it's somewhat appropriate ... not under or over challenged.

under challenged

> *micro-managing* ... stunts growth and hurts motivation. People want to contribute, so allow them to, it ignites them. You gain from their sense of ownership even if you could fix it quicker.

> *over-loading* ... a co-worker does a task well and so gets dumped on. It's proficient, but soon not a challenge. Their expertise got them more than they wanted. Burn out may be near.

over challenged

> *over stretch* ... you can give someone more than they can handle or more than their confidence will allow at the moment. Stay involved enough to read their energy level. If you see red flags ... ask, listen, offer your perspective, look for ways to accommodate their needs.

> If their performance drops ... your first check is to find what might be causing that, and looking for ways that they could be under or over challenged is an important check to make.

Part 4

Applying Adaptive Coaching

13 – Analyzing Performance Levels
14 – Performance Coaching
15 – AC Performance Management

In Part 4, we'll look at how to make use of the AC model ... both in day to day situations (Performance Coaching) ... and with a broader development plan (Performance Management).

Before we can match coaching appropriately, we've first got to be able to analyze where a co-worker is. We'll discuss that process first.

13 Analyzing Performance Levels

A doctor that applies good medicine but for the wrong ailment is not helping. In a similar way, excellent coaching misapplied is not excellent, it's a hindrance. So, we are no more effective than our ability to analyze needs.

Sometimes we identity needs pretty well intuitively. But it's important to have a thoughtful process to check our instincts, and to overrule them as needed. This chapter will present a simple process for analyzing performance. But first of all, let's get clear on what we rating.

we rate:

current performance … how they are performing in the present … not where they were in the past, or what potential they may have.

of a specific task … each task gets its own rating because expertise varies and often does not transfer. Being an expert in one task does not make someone an expert in another.

We are NOT rating past performance, future potential, or overall performance.

+ / − rating system

For a specific task ... we'll rate all 3 factors with a plus or minus as a compass to find our way in matching coaching with needs. The combination of these marks will point us to Performance Level 1,2, or 3.

Competence	*Confidence*	*Motivation*

+ means YES, that factor is **significantly present**

− means NO that factor is not **significantly present**

Identifying Performance Level gives us an intelligent place to start. Continue to analyze the situation. Adjust as you see evidence.

The goal of analyzing performance is to identify Performance Level (PL). Let's see what to look for to determine PL.

- Level 3 = Yes to all 3

    Only when each of the 3 are **significantly present**, do you delegate.

- Level 2 = Yes to competence, but a minus on one other.

    Joe has demonstrated competence in this task, yet either confidence or motivation is not **significantly present**. Thus, it's not yet time to delegate. You are in between Delegating and Directing ... thus Facilitating.

- Level 1 = No to competence, which alone determines PL 1

    The others are good to know, but will not shift the PL.

	Competence	Confidence	Motivation
3 successful	+	+	+
2 moderate	+	-/+	-/+
1 unsuccessful	—	-/+	-/+

seeing patterns

Maybe seeing patterns may help you grasp the logic and soon use it with ease. Take 30 seconds to focus on the shaded areas looking for patterns.

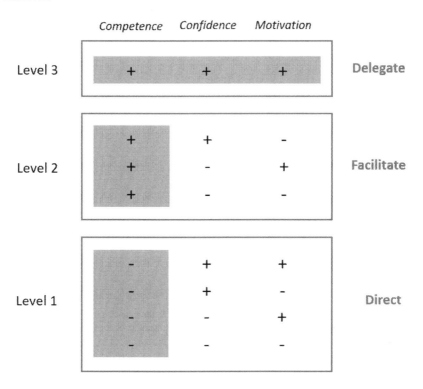

Let's look at level 1 for a moment. When competence is inadequate, focus there first. Delay concerns about confidence and motivation, because improved performance may likely impact them both.

When performance improves, but confidence or motivation does not, you are now at Level 2 ... and facilitating around issues of confidence and / or motivation.

When all 3 are significantly present, delegate, don't be a hindrance.

If you get stuck on how to rate a person's 3 factors ... this detail is added to help you think it through a bit more. But, don't make this process too complicated. Keep it simple, less is more. Try to go with your gut and stick with the simpler method.

	Issue	Rate: + / -
Competence	**Task Knowledge** *understands how*	
	Task Skills *is now doing*	
	Task Resources *has what's needed*	
Confidence	**Experience** *has done this before*	
	Plan *understands the steps necessary*	
	Belief in Self *has assurance in own ability*	
Motivation	**Vision** *sees big picture & understands consequences*	
	Reason *is personally connected to results*	
	Undistracted *no unresolved personal or interpersonal issues?*	

Note*: Remember that Confidence and Motivation are internal, a state of mind. Before you make any significant interventions, make sure to verify your assumptions.*

14 Performance Coaching

Now let's create an easy to use coaching plan for an individual, Joe Sample. Joe is on your team. His role has multiple tasks. Each task has its own goal or expectation.

Let's look specifically at how you have rated Joe on each task and how to coach him accordingly.

Key Tasks	C	C	M	= PL
Writing Reports	+	-	+	2
Giving Presentations	-	+	+	1
Organizing Systems	+	+	+	3
Marketing Programs	-	+	-	1

Task: Writing Reports

Joe has done accurate reports for you in the past, not perfect but pretty well done. He has shown the ability to get details accurate. These next reports however, are of a broader scope and will be seen by those higher up, not just you. He's eager to get it right, but unsure how much detail and formality is needed at this next level.

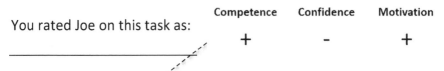

	Competence	Confidence	Motivation
You rated Joe on this task as:	+	-	+

Your rating puts Joe at Level 2 for this task, your style is *Facilitate*, and your initial Focus is around *Confidence*.

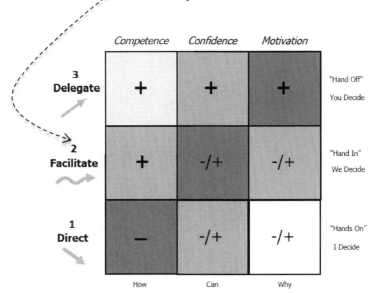

	Competence	Confidence	Motivation	
3 **Delegate**	+	+	+	"Hand Off" You Decide
2 **Facilitate**	+	-/+	-/+	"Hand In" We Decide
1 **Direct**	—	-/+	-/+	"Hands On" I Decide
	How	Can	Why	

Your coaching: Lead with questions and discussion. Offer suggestions, and when he asks for guidance, turn the question back on him to get his opinion before giving yours. Remind him of his competence using examples. Stay connected on how the reports are coming. Let him feed off of your confidence in him.

Task: Giving Presentations

Joe seems to be comfortable in front of people. He's comfortable with the attention and looks for opportunities to be on stage. The problem is, Joe gets way off topic. His focus wanders and he loses people. He has good things to say, if you can hang on for him to wrap it all up. But not enough of his audience can, and that's an issue.

You rated Joe here as:	Competence	Confidence	Motivation
	−	+	+

Your rating puts Joe at Level 1 for this task. Your style is *Directive*, and your initial focus is on *Competence*.

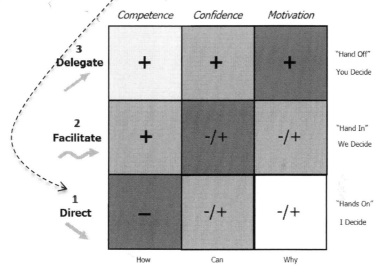

Your coaching: Joe needs you closely involved to tighten up his next presentation to help keep people's attention. Help him with the 'how to' part of preparing a well thought out script, and then sticking to it. Watch him practice it and give specific feedback. Remind him of your confidence in him in the areas he does well in.

Task: Organizing Systems

Joe's role also requires that he provide structure for others to minimize redundancy. Joe is an organizer. If you walk into his office, you can quickly see that order is important to him. This translates well into his team responsibilities where he is in charge designing systems that make the project flow smoothly.

You rated Joe here as:

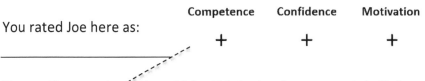

	Competence	Confidence	Motivation
	+	+	+

Your rating puts Joe at Level 3 for this task, where your style *Delegate*, and your initial focus is on *Motivation.*

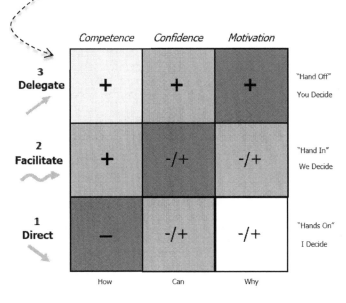

Your coaching: Joe does this very well, so let him have some room to figure out how to get there. Be clear on the overall objectives he is responsible for, and stay available, but let his ideas play out. Keep an eye out that he doesn't get overloaded with these type tasks just because he does them well.

Task: Marketing Programs

A key aspect of Joe's role is to market and sell programs. It's essential to this small company. Joe knows that he connects easily with others, and that he understands needs and solutions well. Yet, currently contracts are not completed often. It appears his attention has been drawn to other tasks and this has been neglected.

	Competence	Confidence	Motivation
You rated Joe here as:	–	+	–

Your rating puts Joe at Level 1 for this task, where your style *Directive*, and your initial focus is on *Competence.*

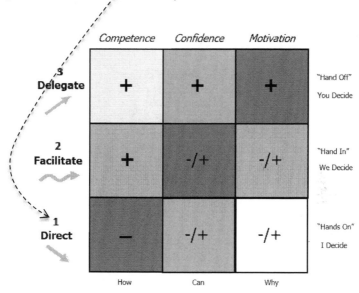

Your coaching: In AC ... competence refers to demonstrated competence ... not potential. The job is not getting done and you have to step in and create change. So, find out what's missing in his sales steps and be clear that you will direct a new process. Give Joe a clear plan to bring about change and be close by. Don't worry about motivation being low now, wait to see if some success begins to change that.

	Competence	Confidence	Motivation
Delegate	Clarify goals and any boundaries, but then stay pretty hands-off regarding details and how-to's. Give them freedom to do things their own way. Monitor overall progress. Make sure they have resources needed.	Show confidence by delegating with little apprehension. Develop atmosphere with freedom to take risks and mistakes are learnings, not fatal. Verbalize in person and in front of others, your confidence in them.	Increasingly connect them to the results of their efforts. Resist overloading - which can de-motivate. Acknowledge contributions and results. Present or listen to their new / next motivating challenges.
Facilitate	Check for understanding of task. Feed their need to know by discussing and clarifying more detail. Get into the whys that go with the how to's. When stuck, ask questions first to engage them. Resist the urge to fix it too soon. Struggle is ok.	Compliment the good. Discuss apprehensions. Express your belief and vision, and why, remind them of successes. Encourage new thinking and risk taking. Make failure a learning experience, not fatal. Share decision making.	Connect them to the results they get. Discuss more of the big picture, vision, and how it matters. Discuss how this task fits with their work values, talents, etc. If in regression ... has success been 'punishing' in any way? (ex: overloaded?).
Direct	Provide clear and patient directions on the specifics of this task. Break into chunks, build progressively. Model the desired behavior. Allow for skill practice with clear and provide specific feedback. Avoid demeaning while correcting.	Confidence will build more from their successes, than your words ... so break skill development into doable steps, don't overwhelm ... Identify apprehensions and provide alternative viewpoint. Find the good, acknowledge progress. Reduce fear of mistakes.	Mention the overall vision and where this task fits / makes its contribution. Clarify impact of success or failure. Avoid long conversations that detract from action. Expect motivation (and confidence) to grow as they experience success.

15 AC Performance Management

Adaptive Coaching – Performance Management (AC-PM) works well with both informal and formal performance management.

The main difference between informal and formal is not so much in the steps, but in how widely used they are.

informal ... is for any team leader who needs a simple and intuitive process to get their people on the same page. Maybe you need it for a current big project. Or, maybe you want greater clarity, accountability, and performance tracking in general ... but there's no company-wide system to latch on to.

Even if you're midstream in a project, getting clarify and agreement on roles and expectations is like pushing a reset button, which we do all the time in life and work. AC-PM can guide you through a needed jumpstart.

formal ... is when a company or department wants a proactive approach to establishing clear roles and expectations, tracking progress, and coaching with a common language clear plan.

Before the Coach / Co-worker conversations happen in Step 2, both will separately put in writing their own answers to the bullet points below.

A) *Role & Task Clarification*
Role
- Your role title:
- The overall objective of this role is:
- How does this role impact our larger company goals?
- In your experience with this role, what have you learned on your own that you wish you had been taught initially?

Task
- List, randomly, the tasks essential in this role
- Rank these tasks in terms of importance (A, B, C etc)
- Assign percentage of your time required (total = 100%)
- List skills necessary in this task
- Clarify what Level 3 performance looks like for each task
- List insights you have gained <u>on each task</u>, that you were not taught going into this role.

B) Task Performance Ratings

Coach and Co-worker rate the Co-worker's performance in each task:

- Coach (C) – uses Performance Level 1,2,3 as discussed in Ch 13
- Co-worker (Co) – (who has not read Ch 13) rates their own performance on the amount of help they feel they need:
  3 = very good ... very little help needed
  2 = okay ... some help needed
  1 = not so good ... a lot of help needed

This information will compare and contrast how both see the role, and how both see the co-worker's performance.

For: Joe Sample		Role Title: Business Development Specialist					
Key Tasks		**Rank**		**PL**		**% Time**	
Coach	Coworker	C	Co	C	Co	C	Co
Marketing Programs	Marketing Programs	A	B	2	3	50	20
Giving Presentations	Presentations	B	C	1	2	10	30
Organizing Systems		C		3		15	
Writing Reports	Documentation	D	D	2	3	25	10
	Customizing Programs		A		2		40

.

Rank = force ranking of each task based on importance perceived
PL = Performance Level ratings
% Time = percentage of time estimated for each task (total = 100)

The next step involves conversations that discuss this information.

Coach / Co-worker Discussion Guide

	Steps	Co-worker	Coach	Both
	Fill out ahead of time Prework A & B			✓
Dialogue A Role & Task Clarification	Share notes on Role & Task Clarification Listen to learn, ask clarifying questions, no disagreements or correcting here	Shares 1st	Shares 2nd	
	Highlight agreements, identify gaps, brainstorm fixes.			✓
	Clarify decisions made (whether jointly or by coach) on how to proceed.		✓	
Dialogue B Task Performance Ratings	Share notes on Task Performance Ratings. Listen to learn, ask clarifying questions, no disagreements or correcting here.	Shares 1st	Shares 2nd	
	Highlight agreements, identify gaps, brainstorm fixes.			✓
	Clarify decisions made (whether jointly or by coach) on how to proceed.		✓	

Note: Separate Dialogue 1 and 2 … because once Task Performance conversation begins it will likely dominate. Give Role and Task Clarification its needed time without distraction.

Step 3 – Coaching Plan

You've now discussed the written notes with your co-worker, whose input may have added a lot to your understanding and shifted some of your initial perceptions. It's time now to close this meeting by being clear as to where you currently stand on:

- their role … its objective and its company contribution
- the role's essential tasks, and % of time demanded
- their performance on each key task
    - tasks that are level 3 … why specifically?
    - tasks below level 3 … what's missing?
- and how you plan to coach them, specific to each task
- key objectives and due dates

Discuss and come to agreement.

Coach Summary Notes

For : Joe Sample   *Date* :   *Role Title*: Business Development Specialist

Rank	Key Tasks	% Time	PL	Key Objectives	Date
A	Marketing Programs	50	2		
B	Giving Presentations	10	1		
C	Organizing Systems	15	3		
D	Writing Reports	25	2		

Schedule the next coaching conversation.

Below is an example of tracking progress. A, B, C, & D are the tasks. They can shift in priority as you see occurred in August.

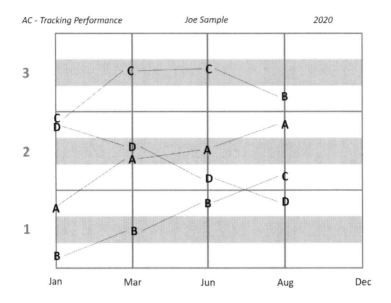

AC - Tracking Performance   Joe Sample   2020

clarify
- agree, in writing, on key expectations, be specific
- agree, in writing, on timeline for all key accomplishments

hold accountable
- check in at key intervals, praise or prod based on the amount of progress, answer questions, be available as needed … the goal is no surprises at crunch time
- when deadlines come … compliment or uphold expectations

follow up
- establish how often Coach Check-in's will occur
- review overall performance, not just specific projects
- as possible, use data to clarify your points and observations

In conclusion

Helping or coaching others in any development effort is a process. Experience is the best teacher for both the coach and the co-worker ... it's how we build wisdom and intuition. Our hope and expectation is that Adaptive Coaching will be a valuable guide and framework to help you apply yours more and more effectively.

Your comments and feedback would be appreciated.

Contact me at Bill@AdaptiveTeamLeadership.com

Made in USA - Crawfordsville, IN
95237_9781736172902
02.18.2021 1833